THE NOVELS OF E. M. Forster

THE NOVELS OF
E. M. Forster

BY JAMES McCONKEY

Archon Books

1971

© 1957 by Cornell University
Reprinted 1971 with permission in an unaltered and
unabridged edition by
The Shoe String Press, Inc., Hamden, Connecticut
International Standard Book Number 0-208-00464-5
Library of Congress catalog card number 74-143882
Printed in the United States of America

TO *Clark Livensparger and Hansford Martin*

Acknowledgments

THE selections from *Where Angels Fear to Tread*, *The Longest Journey*, *A Room with a View*, and *Howards End* are used with the permission of Alfred A. Knopf, Inc. The selections from *Aspects of the Novel*, copyright, 1927, by Harcourt, Brace and Company, Inc., and renewed, 1955, by E. M. Forster, and the selections from *A Passage to India*, copyright, 1924, by Harcourt, Brace and Company, Inc., and renewed, 1952, by E. M. Forster, are used with the permission of the publishers. The selection from *D. H. Lawrence's Letters to Bertrand Russell* is used with the permission of the Viking Press and Gotham Book Mart.

Contents

CONTENTS

1 ⟂

Introduction

ALTHOUGH he has published only five novels, the most recent, *A Passage to India*, appearing as long ago as 1924, E. M. Forster maintains a high rank among the writers of fiction in the twentieth century. Yet for a writer whose works have been consistently accepted as among the best the first half of the century has produced, it is remarkable how inadequate has been the criticism dealing with him. Of the two full-length studies which have been devoted to Forster, the first, Rose Macaulay's *The Writings of E. M. Forster* (1938), is less a work of criticism affording the reader a fuller insight into Forster than it is a graceful appreciation. The other study is that of Lionel Trilling, which, published in 1943, helped to develop a new burst of enthusiasm for Forster and coincided with the republication of those novels of his which had been out of print. But, in examining Trilling's *E. M. Forster*, one needs to keep constantly in mind that Trilling is reading Forster primarily as a kind of guidebook for the modern liberal; such a reading explains, for example, why he finds *Howards End*, rather than *A Passage to India*, to be Forster's masterpiece, and why he dismisses the final section of that latter novel with little more than the statement that it is difficult to know what to make of its "dominant Hinduism." The final result is that Trilling presents a wise and provocative discussion of liberalism which—in spite of the liberalism to be found within Forster—misses much of the essential matter of the novels: the novelist at times slips away and leaves the critic to a discussion of his own particular beliefs.

Trilling's study suggests, I think, that the critic cannot approach Forster as he is apt to approach other novelists. For the critic, unfortunately or not, often tends to turn feeling into idea in order to convey meaning, and to dismiss what cannot be so converted; yet when one attempts to assign to Forster an idea or set of ideas in order to arrive at the explanation of his values, Forster displays a most irritating elusiveness. On one level, of course, the critic intent on ideas finds him far from elusive: *A Passage to India*, so long as it is viewed only as a discussion of the racial problem in India as that problem involves the English colonizers, is a remarkably simple novel; and *Howards End*, viewed as the attempt of the imaginative liberal concerned with

the life of inner values to achieve a harmonious relation with the businessman concerned with externals
and the life of action, is a novel nearly as direct.

The portion of Forster's novels which deals essentially with the world of human relationships, the world
of human reality, is not difficult to analyze; and it is
indeed an important element in his fiction. That it is
but a portion, however, and that the world of human
reality is ever contrasted with another reality any
reader of him is aware. Forster's interest in both the
human and transcendent realities accounts for what his
friend G. Lowes Dickinson has termed his kind of
"double vision," a sense of "this world, and a world or
worlds behind." These "worlds behind" cannot be ignored or given a minor position by the critic, for in
Forster the sense of the transcendent realm consistently affects and colors the physical realm. Yet the
transcendent and physical realms are always distinct,
and his protagonists do not embody any transcendent principle as does, say, Heathcliff in *Wuthering
Heights*. Rather, the Forsterian hero is incomplete, that
incompleteness being the result of a dissociation between the character and his universe, between the individual in a seemingly chaotic, temporal world and the
unifying, eternal reality. This latter reality is "there,"
whether one sees it or not; but the point is that the
individual does *not* see it, cannot verbalize upon it or
make it concrete, for he cannot approach it rationally.
Feeling may inform him of an eternal unity, but the
sense of his identification with that unity is normally

denied him; indeed, the fact that he may, now and then, apprehend the transcendent within the temporal makes the gulf seem even wider, the division of real and ideal more intense. Man in the Forsterian world is no microcosm: the unconscious faith of the Elizabethan hero in his identification with the universe and with divinity— a faith out of which he asserts his unbound individuality—is not present in Forster's heroes. Thus the importance in Forster of reason as well as of feeling: the latter to keep the individual aware of the existence of the transcendent; the former, subservient to feeling, to allow him to select and choose in the temporal world in order that he may achieve what harmony is possible.

Forster is hence not a mystic; nor is he, on the other hand, the novelist of ideas, though he has been praised for, and accused of, being both. The voice we hear as we read him is not that of one who has pierced the heavens, nor that of one whose primary intent is to discuss the ideas needful for our proper existence on earth; it is rather that of a mediator, neither God nor man, who carries on from a mid-point between the two: knowing less than one, sensing more than is normally possible for the other. In his own study of longer fiction, *Aspects of the Novel*, Forster comments on two occasions on the authorial voice in the novel form. As far as the story itself—the narrative of events in their time sequence—is concerned, that voice, he thinks, "does not give us anything as important as the author's personality"; what it does "is to transform us from readers into listeners, to whom 'a' voice speaks, the voice of the tribal narrator, squatting in the middle of the cave, and saying one thing after another until the audience falls asleep among their offal and bones." But voice in fiction, he suggests in the later chapter entitled "Prophecy," may possess a significance which goes far beyond such a primitivistic level: there may be a *tone* to the voice, it may possess an accent which is uniquely its own and which will make its effect upon the entire novel. That tone or accent relates to the author's state of mind as he composes. The Forsterian voice—an unfortunately pretentious term, though one for which it is difficult to find a substitute—clearly possesses such a tonal quality. It is, indeed, so important an element in all five novels that it assumes the dimensions of an ever-present major character; the reader is as aware of the voice in *Howards End* and *A Passage to India* as he is of Margaret Schlegel and Fielding. And, possessing as it does the compassion combined with the remove, the detachment, which one normally associates with the Christian saint or the devout Brahman, that voice reveals a major aspect of the author's own vision. The Forsterian voice, as we sense it, is to a large extent the result of a point of view which focuses upon the characters from the mid-point: the unique effect of Forster, in fact, comes from his mediation as voice, detached, perhaps painfully, from the physical and transcendent worlds, aware of the incompleteness of his people and the completeness beyond them. Since the physical and transcendent worlds are apparently so disparate, and since the mediator cannot unlock the secret of the latter for us, the chief means at his disposal are symbolic ones. Forster's symbols are intended to suggest and imply the relation, so dimly perceived by us, between us and the transcendent.

The most suitable method of coming to critical terms with Forster would thus seem to be through a study of that voice and those symbols. Certainly Forster's use of symbols is the richest and most intricate aspect of his art and gives to the novels an effect not unlike that of music. Forster has remarked that "music is the deepest of the arts and deep beneath the arts," and music affords him a basic analogy to fiction throughout *Aspects of the Novel*. Like music, Forster says, fiction may contain rhythm. That rhythm may be repetition with variation of a phrase or an image, the repetition imparting an effect that goes beyond the specific phrase or image; or it may be the final expression of the novel as a whole after it has been read, creating an effect similar to that produced by Beethoven's Fifth Symphony, "where, when the orchestra stops, we hear something that has never actually been played" —something which proceeds mainly from the inter-relationship of the major parts of the work. In either case, rhythm is an important factor in the production of beauty in the novel form and helps give to it a sense of expansion. Forster continually returns to this matter of expansion in *Aspects of the Novel;* it is, he says,

the idea the novelist must cling to. Not completion. Not rounding off but opening out. When the symphony is over we feel that the notes and tunes composing it have been liberated, they have found in the rhythm of the whole their individual freedom. Cannot the novel be like that?

His own fiction, certainly, makes the attempt. The primary effort of Forster in *The Longest Journey* and *Howards End*—his two most ambitious novels before *A Passage to India*—is to effect some kind of reconciliation between the human and transcendent realms through the Forsterian voice, through the author at mid-point, the implication of the final oneness of the realms being made chiefly by means of rhythmic imagery dealing with the earth and the mysterious flux of nature. In *The Longest Journey*, published in 1907, trust is given to the instinctual man, one who is close to the earth and who thus—like some of D. H. Lawrence's characters—is devoid of hypocrisy and capable of right relations with other men: he is a kind of Pan, a pagan with a strong physique; and he, through his progeny, is to inherit the earth. By the time of *Howards End* (1910), the emphasis on the completely instinctual man has decreased, and attention centers on Margaret Schlegel, an intelligent member of the middle class to whom imagination and the "inner" life are important. It is the novel's intent that Margaret obtain a harmonious relation in marriage with Henry Wilcox, a businessman whose concern, as has already been suggested, is with action and the "outer" life. Margaret, in accomplishing a spiritual connection with Henry, is aided primarily through place—through Howards End, the ancestral home of Henry's first wife, Ruth; and through the spirit of the deceased Ruth Wilcox

7

herself. In *The Longest Journey* and *Howards End*, the earth represents the continuity which exists within the eternal change of nature; it provides the means whereby man can perceive his connection with his ancestors and with all the past as well as with his fellows. Both novels utilize a powerful series of repetitive symbols to suggest the mystery of the eternal natural flux and man's relation to that flux.

Yet neither novel, regardless of what praise one must rightfully give it, is wholly successful. To use Forster's own criteria, each novel develops an expanding imagery based on the repetition of symbols, but neither fully gains the liberation and sense of final expansion which Forster obviously desires to impart to it. In both cases, the reason relates directly to that consideration basic to all the novels, the Forsterian voice.

In *The Longest Journey*, that voice is to a large extent responsible for the reader's mixed reactions at the conclusion. The novel is Forster's only tragic one—at least in the sense that it is the only novel in which the protagonist meets both death and despair; but the finality which always has been an accepted aspect of tragedy is foreign to Forster's way of feeling, foreign to the mind which operates in awareness of the eternal as well as of the temporal. Basically, a major flaw of the novel is a voice that is imperfect, not yet completely controlled: we as readers become too subjectively immersed in the protagonist, Rickie Elliot. There is, it is true, a voice above us; it delineates the people with a love and a compassion; it indicates that they are fragments of completion; but it also descends and becomes both mediator *and* Rickie Elliot. As a result, we become so identified with him that we won't accept his death in the proper spirit; we demand the greater dignity which finality (but not Forster) can provide. Do we not, in spite of his intended personal appeal, actually resent the happiness given in the epilogue to Stephen Wonham, Rickie's half brother and the man close to earth? The epilogue is intended to merge the present with the infinite, to impart the sense of a divine order with which man can effect a harmony; but the conclusion fails to satisfy, and as a result there is no full sense of an "opening out."

In *Howards End* the problem is somewhat different. Here the voice is more carefully controlled; it maintains its position at mid-point. But what happens is that the chief character, Margaret Schlegel, ultimately assumes the solitary position of the voice and thereby weakens her connection with the physical world. Thus the intended reconciliation of the physical and transcendent is imperfect and the novel fails fully to "open out."

In this respect it is pertinent to note that, in spite of its attempt at mediation, the Forsterian voice has always been in at least partial opposition to the Forsterian thematic suggestion that man, through earth and place, can obtain a harmonious relation with other men and with the rest of the physical world. For whenever his characters have gained the experience and intuitive power necessary for such a harmonious relation, they begin to mount to that solitary and detached position which is also their author's. In Forster's first published novel, *Where Angels Fear to Tread*, Philip Herriton's progression is from an amused snobbism to a wise, though lonely, detachment from human reality. In *Howards End* Margaret Schlegel does not, through marriage, lessen the gap between herself and the rest of humanity but becomes a person more detached from that world—a compassionate spectator who is nurse and moral guardian to Henry Wilcox.

We sense a universality in Forster's writings only when he implies man's inability to perceive his oneness with the universe. Only then do we sense the greatness of compassion emanating from that solitary voice above us. Forster writing of an actual harmonious relation among men or between man and his universe is not much more than an interesting stylist with a difficult thesis. Concerned though he is with the world of human relations, Forster's particular perception of that world proceeds from his detached position, from his refusal or his inability to enter actively into those relations. It is such a dilemma which accounts not only for the Forsterian voice, but for the sadness which permeates the three major novels (*The Longest Journey*, *Howards End*, and *A Passage to India*) and lurks behind the comedy of the other two (*Where Angels Fear to Tread* and *A Room with a View*); and certainly his acknowledgment of that dilemma is central to the expansion achieved in his final novel.

For the major difference between *Howards End* and

that last novel, *A Passage to India*, lies in Forster's final awareness of the incompatibility of the position of his voice and the world of human relations. Obviously the solution provided in *Howards End*—that, through place, an individual involved within the confusion and change of human relations can achieve the same insight as that which Forster, from his remote mid-point, can achieve—is in *A Passage to India* found wanting. Partly, the reason is not to be found within Forster himself at all; it is simply that man, in the years between the publication of the two novels, has completed the process of alienating himself from earth: cosmopolitanism has severed man's connection with a specific locality, and science has invalidated even more fully than it had previously the sense of a divine cosmic order in which earth, and hence man, partakes.

Regardless of contributing reasons, in *A Passage to India* Forster has written a novel in which voice, instead of opposing the other aspects of the work, manages to enrich and substantiate them; and the full measure of the success of the novel, in contrast with the partial success of *Howards End*, suggests that Forster has finally come to terms with himself and his universe. Those terms are predominantly the ones which voice has suggested from the time of *Where Angels Fear to Tread*, and they are imparted to us most completely in the last novel through the character of Professor Godbole, the Brahman Hindu. Godbole is the only person in all the novels who becomes the character-equivalent of the Forsterian voice. His position is one of detachment from human reality and from the physical world, a detachment obtained by as complete a denial of individual consciousness as is possible, that denial and remove bringing with them a sense of love and an awareness of unity. For him, as for the Forsterian voice, a full perception of the transcendent reality is impossible, as is a full awareness of the unity within the physical world; but his achievement, though partial, though won only by renunciation, is still a victory, and the only victory that mankind, divorced from a friendly earth, can achieve.

The major symbology of the novel falls within the Hindu frame of reference and achieves a most beautiful and intricate rhythmic expansion: *A Passage to India* by itself justifies all of Forster's attempts to transfer that quality of music to fiction. The central symbol of the Marabar Caves, which has so often perplexed the reader of Forster, becomes more explicable, though still no less the mystery it is intended to be, when the reader perceives the emptiness of the caves to be, on one level, a representation of the absolute Brahman in Hindu philosophy—empty, devoid of attributes, the ultimate reality beyond time and space and hence beyond human comprehension, with which the individual soul will finally merge. It is no wonder, then, that in *A Passage to India* the Marabar makes its effect even in the opening pages; that its hills and caves are related intricately to all the other major imagery of the novel; and that, in contrast with the Marabar, the world of human relations and the physical universe itself seem ultimately illusory.

But above and beyond all individual rhythmic symbology, the novel as a whole possesses a rhythm, its three sections—as one of Forster's critics, the late E. K. Brown, has noted—constituting a rising, a falling, and a rising again which is also a return. It is the magic of *A Passage to India* that we sense the beginning of a new cycle, that we sense the order beyond the cycle, without an explicit last-moment projection of it for us. Projection is there, but it requires no Stephen Wonham sleeping out at night upon the earth with his child; it requires no comment from Margaret Schlegel regarding the future—and no too-rapid and implausible harmonizing of human relations, like that in both *The Longest Journey* and *Howards End*. It is achieved, really, through an *exclusion* of present humanity altogether. A new pattern will evolve, we know, a new cycle and then another; but it is the curving of the cycle we are aware of finally, not the characters of Fielding or Aziz or even of Godbole. Such is not only the sadness and inevitable sense of loss which the Forsterian voice involves, but such also is its vision of love and unity; for *A Passage to India* marks the perfection of a technique and a philosophy, the perfect union of rhythm and voice.

A final note is needed in connection with the method utilized in this study of Forster. With the aid of pertinent material from Forster's own *Aspects of the Novel* the following chapters develop more fully the points outlined here. W. Somerset Maugham on more than one occasion has announced his suspicions of all critical theories devised by a novelist: "I have never known them to be," he says in *A Writer's Notebook*, "anything other than a justification of his own shortcomings." The comment is somewhat too facile; yet it does suggest that the study of a writer's own critical theories may provide an insight into at least that writer's own fiction. Such a relation of his theories to his novels has provided invaluable aid in this study of Forster, and the titles of the following chapters—"People," "Fantasy and Prophecy," and "Rhythm"—have been chosen from those sections of *Aspects of the Novel* which are most illuminating in reference to his own work.

2 ⌒

People

CHARACTERS in fiction, E. M. Forster tells us in
Aspects of the Novel, are "often engaged in treason
against the main scheme of the book. They 'run away,'
they 'get out of hand': they are creations inside a creation, and often inharmonious towards it"; they are, in
short, "full of the spirit of mutiny."

And Forster goes on to describe two of the devices at
the author's disposal—it is an unusual subject for him,
since he normally displays little interest in the subject
of technical aids for the writer—whereby he can quell
the mutiny and put the people in their proper places.

The first device is the creation of two general types
of characters, the "flat" and the "round." Flat characters, Forster observes in a well-known passage,

were called "humours" in the seventeenth century, and are sometimes called types, and sometimes caricatures. In their purest form, they are constructed round a single idea or quality: when there is more than one factor in them, we get the beginning of the curve towards the round. The really flat character can be expressed in one sentence such as "I never will desert Mr. Micawber."

In contrast to the flat character, the round is capable of change; composed of more than one ingredient, it "is capable of surprising in a convincing way. If it never surprises, it is flat. If it does not convince, it is a flat pretending to be round. It has the incalculability of life about it—life within the pages of a book."

Such a distinction doubtless is of value to the general reader of fiction; but—since we are concerned with the insights provided by the relation of Forster's theories to his novels—does it contribute to our knowledge of Forster's own creations? Lionel Trilling says it does not tell us anything about Forster's own best characters— Ansell in *The Longest Journey*, for example: "Like the appealing Ralph Touchett of Henry James's *Portrait of a Lady*, Ansell is neither flat nor round but *fragrant*." Trilling is not so much arguing the supremacy of the olfactory to the optic nerve as receiving apparatus for appraising character as he is suggesting, perhaps, that Ansell's characterization is chiefly memorable for a pervasive grouping of qualities, not for a dimension.

That the objection has validity is suggested, I think, not only by the portrayal of Ansell but by that of the redemptive figures of the last two novels, Ruth Wilcox

of *Howards End* and Mrs. Moore and Professor Godbole of *A Passage to India*. None of these characters
can be placed with any measure of success into a dimensional category; rather, the impression given by all three
is one imposed in terms of the particular *values* they
possess—values which relate, in one way or another, to
those held by their author. For that matter, none of
Forster's major characters can be liberated from their
creator: if they seldom engage in mutinous acts against
his books, the reason is not that he has categorized them
neatly as flat or round, but that they have been constructed to represent a portion of his own insight, to
suggest a portion of that vision which the novel as a
whole represents.

Forster's remarks about the second device are of more
immediate interest, for they relate, if imperfectly, to his
own writing techniques; and they reveal a characteristic
attitude. The device is that of point of view—the particular focus utilized by the author in presenting his
narrative, a matter involving his choice of the mind, or
minds, through which the material of the story is to be
presented.

It is Forster's belief that a writer should be free to
shift viewpoint from character to character, and from
character to his own omniscient or semiomniscient
position, whenever he desires; the chief thing that matters is his power "to bounce the reader into accepting
what he says." The comment is directed against all critics who, in the interest of form, would limit the use of
point of view to a "fixed" focus. It is utilized specifically

as a rebuttal to Percy Lubbock's *The Craft of Fiction*, a book which holds viewpoint to be the essence of method in fiction and which finds in Henry James a complete mastery of the use of viewpoint.

In the light of Forster's espousal of the shifting viewpoint, we might not at first glance expect him to disagree with Lubbock's remarks regarding the use of point of view in *The Ambassadors*. Lubbock considers James's use of the device in this novel to be perfect—perfect because it *does* shift. But it is "an insidious shifting" according to Lubbock, one which is "so artfully contrived that the reader may arrive at the end without suspecting the trick." Even though we apparently see through the eyes of the viewpoint character (Strether), James, without intruding himself in the novel, dramatizes what Strether himself cannot see—his own mind; and James is successful with the subterfuge, Lubbock says, because he lets us see only a fraction, just the obvious amount which any other observer or viewpoint character *might* have seen from the outside. James thus lets the story be revealed gradually and dramatically.

Forster's lack of admiration for the above technique is obviously related to a matter which he never mentions except by implication—the problem of distance. Distance is to a large degree connected with, and the result of, the author's use of viewpoint. It corresponds more or less to the space between the microscope and the material placed on the slide: when the author's "microscope" is close to his "slide," we view a smaller portion of material than we do when the author moves it farther away.

It is precisely through the "insidious shifting," so carefully manipulated, that necessary distance is obtained by James: he turns the lifting knob of the microscope, but only once or twice so that we won't notice. When we compare a Forster novel with *The Ambassadors*, we notice that the turns, so carefully concealed by James, are altogether unnecessary. The microscope is farther removed, the author focuses on a larger area, moves from one character to another, and no trick is needed at all.

That the microscope *is* farther away, though, suggests that despite Forster's obvious dislike for a fixed point of view, he actually does utilize one. If Forster apparently is free to shift from character to character, the reason is that the *real* point of view—that of the detached author—remains unaltered. When he elects to turn over the proceedings to Margaret Schlegel or Mrs. Moore, that point of view still maintains its control over them: a fact which helps to explain why his characters are always colored by their author's own values.

Here, for example, is a passage from *Howards End*. The viewpoint character for the moment seemingly is Charles Wilcox, son of the businessman who is soon to marry Margaret Schlegel; the thought of the forthcoming marriage is depressing to Charles, for reasons soon made obvious:

He strolled out on to the castle mound to think the matter over. The evening was exquisite. On three sides of him a little river whispered, full of messages from the west; above his head the ruins made patterns against the sky. He carefully reviewed their dealings with this family, until he fitted

Helen, and Margaret, and Aunt Juley into an orderly con-
spiracy. Paternity had made him suspicious. He had two
children to look after, and more coming, and day by day they
seemed less likely to grow up rich men. "It is all very well,"
he reflected, "the pater saying that he will be just to all, but
one can't be just indefinitely. Money isn't elastic. What's to
happen if Evie has a family? And, come to that, so may the
pater. There'll not be enough to go round, for there's none
coming in, either through Dolly or Percy. It's damnable!"
He looked enviously at the Grange, whose windows poured
light and laughter. First and last, this wedding would cost a
pretty penny. Two ladies were strolling up and down the
garden terrace, and as the syllables "Imperialism" were wafted
to his ears, he guessed that one of them was his aunt. She
might have helped him, if she too had not had a family to
provide for. "Every one for himself," he repeated—a maxim
which had cheered him in the past, but which rang grimly
enough among the ruins of Oniton. He lacked his father's
ability in business, and so had an ever higher regard for
money; unless he could inherit plenty, he feared to leave his
children poor.

These ostensibly are Charles's thoughts—with the
exception, perhaps, of a portion of the last sentence.
But are they really his thoughts at all, in anything but
the most superficial sense? It is obvious, I think, that
Charles is not the one who finds the evening "exquisite."
He is too insensitive, too much the materialist, ever to
respond to nature; and that, of course, is the point. It is
not *he* who finds the little river's whisperings to be "full
of messages from the west"; if his hearing were attuned
to the frequency required to receive such messages, he
would be a different and more admirable man than he is

—not the sort of man who is concerned with petty suspicions that his father has been duped and that the Schlegels have conspired to keep him, Charles, from his just inheritance. And is it Charles himself who recognizes that the root of his suspicions lies in the fact of his paternity? Hardly. For the point of view is not Charles's after all; he has been observed and interpreted from a position above him.

Almost any passage in Forster's novels would provide similar results, if we chose to analyze it. Forster may shift his attention from character to character, but he does so by viewing them all from a remove: the focus that he employs requires the maintenance of an established distance from the characters and their world. That focus is the basis of all his irony; it is central to his "double vision"; and without it, of course, we could never hear the unique accents of the Forsterian voice.

Major Characters:
Detachment and Incompletion

One senses, in reading Forster, that the author's insight into the world of human relations is a result of his detachment from those relations. His use of point of view, at any rate, makes us feel that not only the irony, but also the compassion and understanding directed upon the major characters come from an observer of, rather than a participant in, human affairs; and it is interesting to note that a similar detachment is developed by those characters who gain a portion of the author's insight—those, that is, who are most aware of the potentialities of life, those most aware of "truth." The detachment of author from characters is paralleled by the feeling of Philip Herriton in Forster's first published novel, *Where Angels Fear to Tread*, that he is fated "to pass through the world without colliding with it or moving it." The novel concerns what we have come to think of as peculiarly Jamesian property: the transplanting of native stock in foreign soil, with the effect of the change being noted by a perceptive observer. In the novel, Sawston concepts of respectability and refinement are modified in the more pagan, instinctual air of Italy.

The reader's interest centers on two people in particular—Caroline Abbott and Philip Herriton. Caroline's sense of social responsibility has caused her to deny her own physical instincts and responses; Philip, the observer, feels untouched by life and somewhat superior to it; he is an aesthetician and humorist turned cynic. The novel's plot involves them in the struggle for a baby, the infant son of the Italian Gino Carella and Lilia Herriton, widow of Philip's elder brother. Lilia, unhappy in marriage to Gino, dies in childbirth; Caroline, chaperone on the trip to Italy which resulted in Lilia's marriage to Gino, considers herself responsible for Lilia's misfortune and determines to bring the baby to England. Such a decision causes Philip's mother to send Philip and his sister Harriet to Italy to bring the child back. Mrs. Herriton wishes simply to maintain the respectability of her family and does not want an out-

sider such as Caroline to perform a duty which so obviously is a family affair.

That the Italian father might have an attachment for
the child, that he might be "filled with the desire that
his son should be like him, and should have sons like
him, to people the earth," none of the English has comprehended. Caroline Abbott is the first to realize that the
child is the center of Gino's life, and she immediately
desists in her attempt to gain it; Harriet, more obdurate
in her narrow feeling of moral and religious duty, kid-
naps the child. Believing only that Gino has sold the
baby to Harriet, Philip accompanies her in a carriage
for the trip to the railroad station, but the carriage overturns and the baby dies.

It is the moment when Philip begins at last to realize
his own involvement and commences the difficult task
of self-redemption. "It was easy to talk of Harriet's
crime. . . . If one chose, one might consider the catastrophe composite or the work of fate. But Philip did
not so choose. It was his own fault, due to acknowledged weakness in his own character." And so, his arm
broken as a result of the accident, he goes to meet Gino,
to whom he confesses his guilt: "It is through me. . . .
It happened because I was cowardly and idle. I have
come to know what you will do." Gino, in sudden
passion, brutally tortures Philip, first twisting his broken
arm and then beginning to choke him. It is Philip's
purgation; Caroline Abbott's entrance prevents it from
becoming his death as well. As she ministers to Philip,

as she comforts Gino in the loss of his son, as she reconciles Philip and Gino, she seems to Philip to be like a goddess.

Many people look younger and more intimate during great emotion. But some there are who look older, and remote, and he could not think that there was little difference in years, and none in composition, between her and the man whose head was laid upon her breast. Her eyes were open, full of infinite pity and full of majesty, as if they discerned the boundaries of sorrow, and saw unimaginable tracts beyond. Such eyes he had seen in great pictures but never in a mortal.

Philip is "saved"; the change which has come over him is one of greater awareness of matters other than refinement. He perceives fully his own involvement in the human tangle, his own responsibility; and he has gained the ability to love. But to achieve his new perspective he must discover a weary and saddening paradox: the all-encompassing view, the one that includes humanity and not merely one's own particular niche, requires the *exclusion* of the individual ego with all its hopes and desires. One is ultimately at a greater remove than ever: Philip sees himself "standing at an immense distance" and must be glad that Caroline, whom he could have loved, "had once held the beloved [Gino] in her arms." The novel ends with Philip still admiring Caroline as goddess, worshiping her; that worship, and the physical passion he *might* have felt for her, are possible only because of the remove, because she is the unattainable vision.

Philip's dilemma is experienced to some extent by most of Forster's protagonists, and the problem is still present in the last novel. To Fielding in *A Passage to India*, "the world . . . is a globe of men who are trying to reach one another and can best do so by the help of good will plus culture and intelligence"; yet Fielding himself is unable to gain a sense of brotherhood with the Moslem, Aziz, at the end of the novel. Politically, the reason is that the English are transgressors on Indian soil; psychologically, it goes deeper than that. Fielding is aware early in the novel that kinship with Aziz is not likely:

"I shall not really be intimate with this fellow," Fielding thought, and then "nor with anyone." That was the corollary. And he had to confess that he really didn't mind, that he was content to help people, and like them as long as they didn't object, and if they objected pass on serenely. Experience can do much, and all that he had learnt in England and Europe was an assistance to him, and helped him towards clarity, but clarity prevented him from experiencing something else.

Personal relations too are hindered by "the spirit of the Indian earth, which tries to keep men in compartments." The mysterious Marabar Hills even suggest to Fielding that human relations are illusory: gazing at the hills at sunset he senses that the conscious self is capable only of a relative, unsubstantial truth and that our essences are but echoes, or reflections, of each other.

Though Fielding after the Marabar episode still believes in the sacredness of personal relations, something has altered; the difference is apparent as he bids goodbye to Adela Quested. Their friendliness is

as of dwarfs shaking hands. . . . When they agreed, "I want to go on living a bit," or, "I don't believe in God," the words were followed by a curious backwash as though the universe had displaced itself to fill up a tiny void, or as though they had seen their own gestures from an immense height—dwarfs talking, shaking hands and assuring each other that they stood on the same footing of insight. . . . Not for them was an infinite goal behind the stars, and they never sought it. But wistfulness descended on them now, as on other occasions; the shadow of the shadow of a dream fell over their clear-cut interests, and objects never seen again seemed messages from another world.

We can make a general statement regarding Forster's people, particularly his male protagonists: their greatest moments are moments, curiously, of simultaneous failure and achievement; their intelligence leads them inevitably to its vanishing point, where intelligence merges with the stars and no longer suffices. What knowledge they have regarding their relation to humanity is obtained through suffering and pain and through their detachment from that humanity. They are finally not complete as human beings, for they are being posited against a concept of universal completion.

In *Aspects of the Novel*, Forster remarks that the major difference between characters in the novel and those in actual life lies primarily in the fact that the writer and reader may possess total understanding of fictional people, while they cannot of actual people. The need for total understanding of a character is a point which the critic is apt to stress, and with which most readers of fiction would be in general agreement; yet the statement requires extensive modification. *Total* understanding is possible only when the writer posits his character against nothing more than a physical reality which exists as a necessary backdrop; the writer and reader can thus see the character in its entirety, for nothing exists but character and backdrop. Forster acknowledges this limitation when he uses Moll Flanders as an example of a creation we "know," one who is before us, complete in every way. He chooses her, indeed, because nothing else intrudes: in Defoe's book "character is everything and can do what it likes."

Forster's own major characters are not liberated in such a fashion; when the reader has learned what he may about their general qualities, their reactions, and their thought processes, he still hasn't learned *all* about them. They are incomplete. Their incompleteness implies completeness, a final integration of man and his universe; but that basic integration must remain to a great extent a mystery, the perception of it limited, as one discovers in *A Passage to India*, to a transitory moment at best. And so we pin Fielding and Philip Herriton as best we can: "round," we say—for they both evolve and are capable of convincing as well as surprising us with their progression—"round but incomplete." The attempt at classification gives us a feeling with Trilling that Forster's best characters are not round at all; but what has intruded is the universe, and the world view of an author who, though capable of frolic and high comedy, is detached, who takes the long view through the microscope and makes us out to be, though dwarfs, rational creatures of essential good will, apt to sense now and then something beyond ourselves that dissatisfies and perplexes.

Major Characters: The Feminine Spirit

Detachment, however, works not wholly as advantage, for one characteristic of Forster's people is a lack of passion and sexual fulfillment. A religiosity colors Forster's major characters, which is perhaps but another way of stating what has already been suggested: Philip Herriton's vision makes of Caroline Abbott a goddess, and though we are told that she—like the goddesses of the Greeks—is capable of physical love, Philip's worship of her is more a self-denying asceticism reminding us of the celibate's love of the Virgin Mother. Though Forster may glorify the physical passion, he does so primarily through his pagan, pastoral people: Gino, the early and uncorrupted Feo of "The Eternal Moment," the carriage driver in *A Room with a View*. Mrs. Moore of *A Passage to India* and Ruth Wilcox of *Howards End* are essentially intuitional, visionary; Gino, Feo, Stephen Wonham, and their *genre*, typically instinctual; the protagonists, such as Philip, Fielding, and Rickie Elliot of *The Longest Journey*, must rely to a larger extent than either of the above groups on intelligence and culture. Only the Ginos can afford intimate relations; the rewards of the others—the visionaries and the protagonists—are mainly the rewards which asceticism and detachment may offer, with the accompanying limitations.

These two latter groups possess related characteristics; they are characteristics which Forster, in *Howards End*, refers to as feminine. Femininity is to be found within the men as well as the women; thus, in *Howards End*, a novel depicting a feminine triumph over a masculine world, the Schlegel household "was irrevocably feminine, even in father's time." Mr. Schlegel we discover to have been an idealist, disdainful of materialism, capable of imaginative encompassment, interested in the "inner" life and personal relationships. These are the attributes of Fielding also, and the fact of their validity the final perception of Philip Herriton; they are, in fact, the attributes of nearly all of Forster's major characters, regardless of sex.

Femininity is a quality, indeed, which tends toward the transcending of the sexual distinction. The movement of the feminine spirit is toward unmeditated love for the whole world and a vision of a realm beyond, a love and vision accompanied by acceptance of self-denial and detachment. The shadows of Ruth Wilcox and Mrs. Moore, brooding over Forster's last two novels, suggest the potentialities of the feminine spirit. The self-denial of both is so complete that they elude not only all dimensional categorization but the distinction of sex itself, existing—as Forster depicts Ruth Wilcox—more as wisps of spirit than as corporeal substance.

The quality in opposition to femininity is, in *Howards End*, represented by all the Wilcox family with the exception of Ruth. Like femininity, masculinity is allied to no concept of sexual completeness; though the Wilcoxes are exceptionally fertile, they are sexually neurotic. The Wilcox attributes are those of action and the "outer" life, of "telegrams and anger"; theirs is the life of materialism, and Forster—so dissimilar to D. H. Lawrence in his depiction of Margaret Schlegel, Ruth Wilcox, and Mrs. Moore—is in agreement with Lawrence that a materialistic society denies sexual fulfillment; Henry Wilcox's secretive early love affair, his shame of bodily passion, are symptomatic. Forster is, of course, in accord with Lawrence in finding that the life of sexuality achieves its liberation in the "natural," instinctive person: Robert, Mrs. Elliot's lover in *The Longest Journey*, suggests the gamekeeper in *Lady Chatterley's Lover*.

But the problem of the protagonists is another matter, not to be solved so simply as is that of Mellors and Constance Chatterley or Robert and Mrs. Elliot. (Lucy Honeychurch's problem in *A Room with a View* is the exception: she has simply denied her natural passions, and when she finally acknowledges and accepts them she achieves a fulfillment as complete as that of any pagan shepherdess.) Unlike such an intuitive character as Mrs. Wilcox, who effortlessly senses the unity encompassing everything in the universe, the protagonists are aware of a perplexing division between the temporal and the eternal realities. Their femininity, in other words, has been developed, but not to the extent that we find it in the intuitive characters: the protagonists sense, though often obscurely, an unseen and transcendent reality, and they have the problem of relating that unseen reality to their own physical existence and to the material world.

For Rickie Elliot and Margaret Schlegel, a reconciliation of the realities is at least theoretically possible; and, indeed, Forster attempts to give Margaret success in achieving such a reconciliation. In the case of Fielding, seen and unseen worlds are far too separated for him ever to perceive a connection between them; his values, nevertheless, are based upon whatever insights of unity, no matter how limited, are granted him, and so his whole concern is personal relationships and the brotherhood of man. All three of these characters are required to apply the insights of the feminine spirit to the outer, masculine, world if they are to achieve their measure of happiness; and they must be prepared to defend those insights against all opposing forces. Like Mr. Schlegel, they must become the "soldiers" of the world; they must be able to "hit out like any ploughboy" (the phrase is Stewart Ansell's) once they have perceived rightly.

But it seems fairly obvious that Rickie and Fielding —and, for that matter, Philip Herriton—are faced with a problem which is psychologically more complex than

Margaret's. No conflict occurs within Margaret, as the feminine spirit in its quest for unity moves her toward self-denial; but in the men we are aware, I think, of a conflict between their sexual nature and the feminine spirit which it is impossible totally to reconcile. They must maintain, in conjunction with their femininity, the separate male identity. It is perhaps not unfair to say of them that their femininity draws them toward a denial of their maleness, but that it is a denial which, psychologically, they are not prepared to make. As a result they can obtain no strong or satisfactory sexual relationships; nor can they achieve, on the other hand, the tranquil state of the individual who has managed to surmount the barrier of sexual differences.

Unlike *The Longest Journey* and *A Passage to India*, *Howards End* is an account of the triumphant power of the feminine spirit in the physical world when that spirit is unhampered by problems of a sexual nature. Margaret's sexuality, such as it is, actually lessens as the novel progresses; through the influence of Ruth Wilcox and Ruth's ancestral home, she gains awareness of the unity beyond all physical divisions. Thus, at Howards End, Margaret perceives the wych-elm outside to be "a comrade. House and tree transcended any similes of sex . . . to compare either to man, to woman, always dwarfed the vision . . . As she stood in the one, gazing at the other, truer relationship had gleamed." Her marriage is a triumph of the feminine spirit, a marriage to which Margaret brings the asexual attributes of self-sacrifice, pity, and compassion. She will marry Henry Wilcox in spite of the degradation to her of his infidelity to his former wife, a degradation implicit in his inability to recognize the very fact of his unfaithfulness. To Margaret, hearing for the first time of that infidelity, "Henry must be forgiven, and made better" by her love—and, one might add, by the general superiority such a remark unfortunately suggests she feels. Margaret's love, certainly, is one which requires as a prerequisite suffering and unworthiness on the part of the recipient.

Henry Wilcox's own problem, involving as it must his reconciliation of masculine with feminine attributes, is never met; any successful reconciliation on his part, for that matter, would be impossible in this novel; for Margaret, like Caroline Abbott, becomes the protecting mother-goddess, a goddess to whom Henry, exhausted through suffering, must turn. There exists consequently a sense of evasion and lack of reconciliation in the novel which becomes especially apparent in the epilogue.[1] Thus, though Trilling is perhaps correct in commenting that in *Howards End* Forster for the first time has shown "the difficulties the truth must meet," and that the novel is hence Forster's first "work of full responsibility," the truth which has been shown and the responsibility which has been met have more the moral than the psychological ring to them. There is to be found in the novel no depth of internal conflict

[1] Other reasons, basically connected with the problem of voice, prevent a full and satisfactory reconciliation in *Howards End*. They are discussed in the following chapter.

—a depth which is found even in *Where Angels Fear to Tread*, which invests *A Passage to India* with such a profound sadness, and which is integral both to the virtues and to the flaws of *The Longest Journey*.

It is an interesting fact that if we are to find an approximate parallel of the protagonist of that latter novel, Rickie Elliot, anywhere else in Forster, it is in a woman, Helen Schlegel, Margaret's sister. Each wants to embrace the world, and to do so will invest its reality with the incorruptible and divine attributes of the unseen world. Also, both are attracted by virility: Helen as she discovers it in Paul Wilcox, Rickie as he divines it in the passionate embrace between Agnes Pembroke and her athlete lover, Gerald Dawes. Rickie, to whom such passion has been unknown, and to whom it is denied, invests the scene with flaming color, and its memory exists with him throughout his own marriage to Agnes. Finally, the deification of this world and its people produces, for each, a distortion: Helen, in compassion for Leonard Bast, will give herself physically to him and will invest him with qualities which are not his; Rickie Elliot will deny his brother, will act out the lie which is to ruin Rickie's own life, and will, furthermore, when he finally *does* accept Stephen, invest in him the absolute qualities of a god.

In what way, one might ask, do the portraits differ? They differ, finally, in the obvious sexual distinction and in the fact that we are occupied more centrally with Rickie and probe into his psychology more profoundly. Distance in this novel has been decreased, not only between Rickie and his world, but between Rickie and his creator. We are so close at times to Rickie that we require a guide; and we are presented with the triumvirate of Stewart Ansell, Anthony Failing, and Stephen Wonham, each of whom represents a concern with a particular aspect of truth.

Ansell, the young Cambridge philosopher, is composed of the sternest stuff, his quest being that of the suprahuman reality. His strength is that he will never impose, as does Rickie, the absolute qualities of that reality upon the world of man. Yet it is the heart, not the head, to which he eventually turns, for "he never forgot that the holiness of the heart's imagination can alone classify" the facts of the world, "can alone decide which is an exception, which an example." Affection he has—for family totally, for friends when they are worthy of it; and he will strike out in action to defend them. Limitations? He is inclined to be pedantic in his view of ultimate reality, his refusal to "see" Agnes being not only perceptive but sophomoric: Agnes, like the cow of the discussion which opens the novel, *is* there, if only on the level of physical reality, and is, as such, a force to be reckoned with. Ansell too, with his family, lacks a sense of taste; his awareness of that deficiency is depicted for us in fine strokes and helps account for the success of his portrayal. His chief deficiencies, one may conclude, are of this world. He is unable to achieve any major reconciliation with it, and his attitude, like the early Philip Herriton's, is one of cynicism: he is never "anything but bored by the prospect of the brotherhood of man."

This is a concept which Anthony Failing, on the other hand, will never desert: "He believed that things could be kept together by accenting the similarities, not the differences of men." Based on man's image, his vision of reality is much less stable than the one which Ansell will seek, and though he loses both his health and the love of his wife, though he blunders along and is widely misunderstood, still "he counted a few disciples in his lifetime, a few young labourers and tenant farmers, who swore tempestuously that he was not really a fool."

Ansell lacks as well, we are told, perception of the reality—though he will sense its validity in Stephen Wonham—which is to be found in the earth itself and which results in an instinctive wisdom that worships the goddesses Artemis, goddess of nature, and Demeter, goddess of fertility. The reality which Stephen represents is the only one of the three capable of fulfillment. Stephen will get drunk, he will throw lumps of clay through windows, he won't understand Rickie's short stories even though their theme is what he himself actually embodies; but he and his assemblage will achieve their destiny.

This, then, is the holy trinity: a divine and incorruptible reality; a reality embodied in mankind; and one which is of the earth and is instinctively divined by the man who is closest to the earth. Rickie Elliot

worships at all three temples of the trinity; his destruction lies in his perhaps inevitable attempt to find a single
symbol to represent them all. If Rickie is weaker than
Ansell, or Tony Failing, or Stephen Wonham, it is,
partly at least, because he attempts more, must accomplish more, and to accomplish more will reveal the in-
nermost operation of his psychology. Hence Rickie is
the character most valuable to us in our analysis of the
protagonists of the other novels: in their relationship
to their world, in their sense of incompleteness in relation to their universe, in their inevitable detachment.

Rickie, in his pursuit of the trinity, is haunted by a
self-pity and a masochism which has at its base a
mother-love accompanied by an awareness of sexual
insufficiency, a latent homosexuality. If, on one level,
Agnes represents to Rickie a goddess of the infinite, on
another she becomes another Gerald, brutal and masculine, who, however frivolously, talks of horsewhipping
Rickie, who has her ears pierced for earrings as symbol
of her betrothal to Gerald and allows him to kiss the
blood on her handkerchief, and who delights in
Gerald's youthful torture of Rickie. Rickie's love for
his mother, related to his own lack of male virility, is
emphasized: because he assumes that Stephen is the il-
legitimate son of his father, he hates Stephen and allows
that hatred to be utilized by Agnes in a denial of
Stephen. That mother-love, which parallels the relationship in other novels of the male protagonists to the
protecting mother-goddesses, later causes Rickie to
turn from Agnes to a love of Stephen when he dis-

37

covers Stephen to be his mother's son, not his father's.

It must be noted, however, that even though these characteristics are obviously to be found within Rickie, the reader cannot with full assurance determine to what extent all of them are deliberately placed there by Forster; the point of view is uncertain, author and Rickie becoming at times so inextricably related that the reader frequently is unable to separate conscious intent from an apparently unconscious authorial self-revelation. Rickie belongs quite clearly to that group of characters who have been constructed out of their authors' own youthful problems and experiences: *The Longest Journey* has, in this respect, elements in common with Butler's *The Way of All Flesh*, Maugham's *Of Human Bondage* and Lawrence's *Sons and Lovers*.

The protagonists of Forster's other novels are more cautious; they will hold themselves intact, knowing that inner chaos may result in their own destruction. Their detachment is partially a safeguard; they will trust human relationships, but they propose a check upon themselves.[2] These other characters attempt less to

[2] That check one may presume to be a major distinction between Lawrence and Forster. The distinction is implied in a letter which Lawrence wrote Bertrand Russell following a three-day visit made by Forster in 1915, a visit which resulted in a quarrel between the two writers. The letter is published in *D. H. Lawrence's Letters to Bertrand Russell*, edited by Harry T. Moore (New York, 1948). An excerpt may suffice:

"Forster is not poor, but he is bound hand & foot bodily. Why? *Because he does not believe that any beauty or any divine utterance is any good any more.* Why? Because the world is suffering from bonds, and birds of foul desire which gnaw its liver. Forster

gain a knowledge of all reality than to make as satisfactory an adjustment as possible between the human world and the overarching harmony, an adjustment which is at best an uneasy balance; which, when achieved, inevitably results in the maintenance of an even greater detachment from that human world where they would like to remain; and which imparts a poignant awareness of loneliness and incompletion.

Minor Characters

We have been dealing with the major characters in Forster, and with the minor ones as they touch upon them. Of the minor galaxy, it is to be noted that questions of adjustment between worlds or between levels of reality offer them no trouble, for they are invested

---

knows, as every thinking man now knows, that all his thinking and his passion for humanity amounts to no more than trying to soothe with poetry a man raging with pain which can be cured. Cure the pain, don't give the poetry. Will all the poetry in the world satisfy the manhood of Forster, when Forster knows that his implicit manhood is to be satisfied by nothing but immediate physical action. He tries to dodge himself—the sight is pitiful.

"But why can't he act? Why can't he take a woman and fight clear to his own basic, primal being? Because he knows that self-realisation is not his ultimate desire. His ultimate desire is for the continued action which has been called the social passion—the love for humanity—the desire to work for humanity. That is every man's ultimate desire & need. Now you see the vicious circle. Shall I go to my Prometheus and tell him beautiful tales of the free, whilst the vulture gnaws his liver? I am ashamed. I turn my face aside from my Prometheus, ashamed of my vain, irrelevant, impudent words. I cannot help my Prometheus. And this knowledge rots the love of activity."

with none of the Forsterian double vision. Concerned only with the world of the physical reality, these minor characters are often the aspirants after "Culture," and their perception is muddied by a devotion, even when they consider themselves singularly free of it, to conventionality. Most of the minor female irritants in Forster's novels are conventionalists: Lydia Lavish, the authoress in *A Room with a View;* Charlotte Bartlett, the chaperone in the same novel; Mrs. Herriton, Philip's mother in *Where Angels Fear to Tread.* If the minor characters possess a moral awareness, it is apt to be an awareness which stems from conventionality: Harriet Herriton is an example, as is the Reverend Cuthbert Eager of *A Room with a View.*

Some of the minor characters carry about with them a slogan: Charlotte Bartlett's is "I know I'm a bother, I'll do what I can not to be"—thereby becoming an intolerable nuisance to Lucy Honeychurch and a comic one to the reader. But to a great extent even the minor characters tend toward roundness. They are round without carrying the world view of their author with them, and the reason for their roundness lies in the psychological outcroppings amid the layer of conventionality or other protective surface. The outcroppings may be of something so secret that it will startle us into acceptance: Mr. Beebe, seemingly so tolerant and sensible, will approve when Lucy Honeychurch breaks her engagement to Cecil Vyse, this approval resulting not so much from a dislike of Cecil as from a concealed belief—no more than a feeling—in celibacy; Agnes Pembroke, who has apparently forgotten Gerald

Dawes in her marriage to Rickie, will be drawn in love to Stephen Wonham because "the poise of his shoulders that morning—it was no more—had recalled Gerald," the love instantly turning to hatred because the secret of her love has been revealed to Agnes herself as well as to Stephen. The hidden may be revealed in a moment of fatigue, as it is with Agnes, Fielding, and Mrs. Moore, when the normal barriers are withdrawn; or it may come, as it does to Cecil Vyse, when the character finds himself in a new situation.

Some stars in Forster's minor galaxy burn more brightly than others. In this number one must include Mrs. Munt—Aunt Juley—of *Howards End* and Mrs. Honeychurch of *A Room with a View*. They of themselves would disprove Montgomery Belgion's thesis—one which has received more attention than it deserves, since that attention results from its singularity alone—that Forster sneers at all those who are outside his elect circle, at all those to whom the spiritual connection is denied. For Mrs. Munt and Mrs. Honeychurch lack the complexity of the major figures, are as unconcerned with the unseen realm as is Mrs. Herriton; they are presented to us primarily because they are necessary to story and plot. One could leave them at that did they not possess one attribute which Mrs. Herriton and the Reverend Mr. Eager do not: the capacity for affection. Mrs. Munt carries her tag—"The Schlegels are as good as any Wilcox." Hers is a familial and racial pride, but it is based on affection, one of the graces that places her with Margaret and Ruth Wilcox. Mrs. Honeychurch muddles along, becomes cross, yet sees that something is wrong with Cecil, who will be superior and uncivil to other people: "No doubt," she tells Lucy, "I am neither artistic nor literary nor intellectual nor musical, but I cannot help the drawing-room furniture; your father bought it and we must put up with it, will Cecil kindly remember." Lacking other logic, Mrs. Munt and Mrs. Honeychurch possess the logic of affection for people and place, and it is through such characteristic expressions as the above that they live for us.

Affection, too, is at the basis of the portrayal of Aziz in *A Passage to India*, affection at once complicated by a psychological insecurity and an apparently innate instability. Aziz will give Fielding the collar button from his own shirt, will honor him by showing him the snapshot of his wife, yet will allow himself to be convinced that Fielding has betrayed him by going to England to marry Miss Quested, having first persuaded Aziz not to collect his fine of twenty thousand rupees.

Aziz did not believe his own suspicions—better if he had, for then he would have denounced and cleared the situation up. Suspicion and belief could in his mind exist side by side. They sprang from different sources, and need never intermingle. Suspicion in the Oriental is a sort of malignant tumour, a mental malady, that makes him self-conscious and unfriendly suddenly; he trusts and mistrusts at the same time in a way the Westerner cannot comprehend. It is his demon, as the Westerner's is hypocrisy.

One other character must be mentioned, for he stands alone in Forster's gallery: Leonard Bast. He represents

Forster's major excursion into the lower middle class, into the realm of those haunted doubly by poverty and culture. His is the dilemma created by modern urban civilization and its concept of Democracy: he might otherwise have possessed kinship with Stephen Wonham or with the woodcutter who, pollarding the churchyard elms as Mrs. Wilcox is being buried, takes a chrysanthemum from her grave to give to his lover. Some obscure impulse from such a heritage sends Leonard on a forlorn, determined expedition into the woods and countryside to escape his basement flat and sordid existence, but he will confuse his trip with the pursuit of culture: he will spew Stevenson and Thoreau and Meredith and will tell the Schlegels that his expedition resulted "from reading something of Richard Jefferies." Leonard, whose "mind and body had been alike underfed, because he was poor," will still proclaim his equality and will prove it through his gentility: a listing of the books he has read and his ability to play Grieg on the piano. "He knew that he was poor, and would admit it," but "he hoped to come to Culture suddenly, much as the Revivalist hopes to come to Jesus." Despite these insights into his nature, Leonard, unlike the majority of Forster's minor characters, never interests us for his own sake. Though he is in *Howards End* so that the picture of the middle class will not omit the poor, his primary function is that of a catalyst: he makes the plot operate by creating problems for the major characters to solve.

3 ◁

Fantasy and Prophecy

THE reader's understanding of a character is, as we have seen, related to the kind of backdrop against which that character is placed: it is possible for us to "know" a character completely only if the backdrop is physical reality alone.

It is this matter of the backdrop which concerns Forster in the chapters titled "Fantasy" and "Prophecy" in *Aspects of the Novel*. The writer of either fantasy or prophecy, he believes, must achieve a liberation from the phenomenal world—a liberation which, in the degree of its achievement, is responsible for his particular vision. Since such a liberation is required, both fantasy and prophecy involve a distortion: a chair, a person, will have a value which is not the value imposed by phenomenal reality. "There is more in the novel than time or people or logic or any of their derivatives, more even than Fate," Forster says in his chapter dealing with fantasy.

And by "more" I do not mean something that excludes these aspects nor something that includes them, embraces them. I mean something that cuts across them like a bar of light, that is intimately connected with them at one place and patiently illumines all their problems, and at another place shoots over or through them as if they did not exist. We shall give that bar of light two names, fantasy and prophecy.

The backdrop utilized by the writer of fantasy and prophecy—the backdrop, that is, which represents a reality distinct from phenomenal reality—Forster refers to as the "mythology" of the work. He finds that the sense of mythology in fantasy and prophecy is the major element of both, while the difference between the two is the difference in the kind of mythology each possesses: "They are alike in having gods," he says, "and unlike in the gods they have." Fantasy, the lower of the pair, deals with anything from Fauns and Dryads to "slips of the memory, all verbal coincidences, Pans and puns." For examples of the use of mythology in fantasy, Forster gives us not only *Zuleika Dobson* but such a novel as *Tristram Shandy* and the early portions of *Joseph Andrews*. The mythology of Sterne's novel is there only by implication—"the deity that lurks behind his masterpiece" is Muddle—and the mythology of *Joseph Andrews* is but another novel, Richardson's *Pamela*. Fantasy, then, includes that which involves, directly or through implication, a double structure; what we see about us is transformed by placing it in operation within another framework, and that second framework is the "mythology." Though the supernatural may be involved, the supranatural is not: "The power of fantasy," Forster remarks, "penetrates into every corner of the universe, but not into the forces that govern it—the stars that are the brain of heaven, the army of unalterable law, remain untouched—and novels of this type have an improvised air, which is the secret of their force and charm."

On the other hand, prophecy to Forster does bear a relation to those forces: partly, at least, because the prophetic writer "has gone 'off' more completely than the fantasist," and "is in a remoter emotional state while he composes." Prophecy is a bardic quality, "a tone of voice" that "may imply any of the faiths that have haunted humanity—Christianity, Buddhism, dualism, Satanism, or the mere raising of human love and hatred to such a power that their normal receptacles no longer contain them." The mythology of prophecy, unlike that of fantasy, suggests unity, a mingling of physical reality with some universal element; and its mythology, whether its deities are Buddha or Christ or are related to no established religion, has no artifice about it, no framework which is *arbitrarily* (and hence intellectually) established around the people and the normal world. To Forster, the reason that prophetic fiction has the bardic quality, bears an affinity with song, is that, though the prophet's "theme is the universe, or something universal," he does not make a direct statement about that universe; he does not necessarily "say" something about it. Rather he merges not only his characters but his readers into that universe through the power of his voice—through, as we have already seen in the initial chapter, the tonal quality of that voice and the accent it possesses. For it is not the belief that counts so much as it is the implication of that belief. The prophet's voice, as Forster perceives it, implies an extension beyond the physical world to a point where barriers and differences are dissipated. Thus Mitya in *The Brothers Karamazov* "does not conceal anything (mysticism), . . . does not mean anything (symbolism), he is merely Dmitri Karamazov, but to be merely a person in Dostoevsky is to join up with all the other people far back."

The Search for a Mythology

It has frequently been remarked that a basic problem of the twentieth-century writer lies in his search for a mythology suitable to contain, to suggest, his own values. The comment, though it has been made less in reference to prose than to poetry, where the use of myth normally becomes more instantly apparent, has a valid application to Forster; for one may follow the development of his fiction in connection with his own search for a suitable mythological referent. His need for such a referent is obvious, since his primary concern as novelist is with the relation of the physical world to the transcendent realm beyond, a realm which may be intuitively sensed but never fully comprehended.

47

Thus it is that the chapters on fantasy and prophecy in *Aspects of the Novel* have a special significance in relation to Forster's own work. Fantasy, largely artifice, inclines toward prankishness and does not require the voice of prophecy, nor nearly so extensive a vision; and, as might be presumed, Forster's progression is from fantasy toward prophecy. If he is to be claimed as a truly prophetic writer, such a claim must ultimately be based upon his last novel, *A Passage to India*. Only in this final novel has Forster found a myth which wholly suits the particular quality of his voice and is in keeping with the unique nature of his vision. The myths he develops in *The Longest Journey* and *Howards End*— the two novels which, with *A Passage to India*, seek a merging into a universal sphere—suggest at times the consciously superimposed mythological framework of fantasy.

His most obvious use of the mythology of pure fantasy, however, is found in the short stories. It is a mythology which stems from earth and nature in general and which represents the interest Forster has had in classical myth since, at least, his years as a Cambridge undergraduate; thus, in the short stories, Pan roams, a girl is a Dryad and turns into a tree to escape her boorish lover (a story which Forster also has Rickie Elliot write in *The Longest Journey*), and a curate meets a Faun in the woods and comes to a realization of his own hypocrisy. In an introduction to the collected edition of his stories published in 1947, Forster points out that not only have there been two major wars since the composition of the stories, but "there are preparations for a third, and Fantasy now tends to retreat, or to dig herself in, or to become apocalyptic out of deference to the atom." But the best of Forster's stories—in this number one must include "The Story of the Siren," "The Celestial Omnibus," and "The Eternal Moment" —require no apology in the age of the atom; rather, as has also been the case with *The Tempest*, they have acquired a heightened significance. In their ironic contrast between human folly and the ideal as that ideal is to be found within nature, they achieve an effect which is akin to Meredith's Comic Spirit, an effect which Meredith himself rarely achieved.

It is interesting to note further that this preoccupation with earth and nature as redemptive agents, so evident in the stories, is carried not only into *A Room with a View*, Forster's only novel which is basically fantasy, but into all the other novels before *A Passage to India*. Though (except in *A Room with a View*) the specific reference to the nature deities of Greek mythology is not so pronounced in the novels as in the stories, the spirit of Pan carries over, as we have seen, into such characters as Gino in *Where Angels Fear to Tread* and Stephen Wonham in *The Longest Journey*. In *Howards End*, Forster—primarily through Ruth Wilcox and to a lesser extent Miss Avery—attempts with partial success to establish characters that embody a peculiarly English mythology. It is in this novel that he asks,

Why has not England a great mythology? Our folklore has never advanced beyond daintiness, and the greater melodies about our country-side have all issued through the pipes of

49

Greece. Deep and true as the native imagination can be, it seems to have failed here. It has stopped with the witches and the fairies. It cannot vivify one fraction of a summer field, or give names to half a dozen stars. England still waits for the supreme moment of her literature—for the great poet who shall voice her, or, better still, for the thousand little poets whose voices shall pass into our common talk.

In his use of classical myth and in his general attitude toward nature and earth as that attitude is found in all the fiction before *A Passage to India*, Forster shows marked resemblance to the English Romantic poets. Especially is this resemblance apparent in the short stories, the most striking example being "The Road from Colonus." The story concerns an Englishman growing old: Mr. Lucas, who, though "he had led a healthy, active life, had worked steadily, made money, educated his children," is now beset with worries of having lived in vain. On a trip to Greece, he finds, far from the normal paths of the tourist, a hollow tree, from which a fountain of water pours; he steps within the hollow part and finds the tokens "to the presiding Power" which others have already left there.

Others had been there before him—indeed, he had a curious sense of companionship. Little votive offerings to the presiding Power were fastened on to the bark—tiny arms and legs and eyes in tin, grotesque models of the brain or the heart—all tokens of some recovery of strength or wisdom or love. There was no such thing as the solitude of nature, for the sorrows and joys of humanity had pressed even into the bosom of a tree.

He presses his body against the tree, closes his eyes, and feels a strange peace; and "he was aroused at last by a shock—the shock of an arrival perhaps, for when he opened his eyes, something unimagined, indefinable, had passed over all things, and made them intelligible and good." He sees, for the first time, meaning in the rustic activities of the country folk in the neighboring fields; and feels kinship with all of humanity.

There was meaning in the stoop of the old woman over her work, and in the quick motions of the little pig, and in her diminishing globe of wool. A young man came singing over the streams on a mule, and there was beauty in his pose and sincerity in his greeting. The sun made no accidental patterns upon the spreading roots of the trees, and there was intention in the nodding clumps of asphodel, and in the music of the water. To Mr. Lucas, who, in a brief space of time, had discovered not only Greece, but England and all the world and life, there seemed nothing ludicrous in the desire to hang within the tree another votive offering—a little model of an entire man.

Thus Mr. Lucas has achieved unity, has found harmony in nature, and has, in the Wordsworthian sense, arrived at philosophical maturity: he has achieved communion with nature and in so doing has achieved communion with man. The realization is the Wordsworthian one of "Nature's holy plan," achieved through contemplation; Mr. Lucas' quest is, as Trilling observes, the Romantic quest, the desire to find meaning and intention in nature, not blind chance or accident. In the last part of "The Road from Colonus," Mr. Lucas returns to London and a tenement and loses completely the perception which he has possessed so brightly; and the day after he leaves, the tree falls over in a windstorm and crushes to death all the occupants of a nearby inn— the inn where Mr. Lucas would have been had he followed his wish and remained. By returning home, he has lost the glory which was transitorily his and which would not have been terminated by death but is terminated by life.

Nature and earth will also act throughout the novels up to *A Passage to India* as unifying forces; but, though they play an important role in each of these novels, one notices a difference in the *kind* of unity which they may afford. Forster, in attempting to establish a mythology suitable to suggest his own values, holds consistently in these four novels to the Romantic quest of finding order in nature and yet gives to that quest an increasingly greater significance: the unifying power of earth is expanded to contain meanings which are far beyond the meanings communicated in his early work.

In the short stories, as in *A Room with a View* and *Where Angels Fear to Tread*, the unity provided by earth is not connected with anything beyond the physical world; though the individual who has achieved harmony with nature as it is manifested on earth has ostensibly achieved harmony with his universe and with divinity, the emphasis never departs from his relation with the phenomenal world and his fellow men. Basically, nature and earth are used in the earlier fiction to afford a reality against which can be contrasted the various methods whereby man defrauds himself:

through his hypocrisy and self-deceit, through his pursuit of "Culture," or through his adherence to convention and standards of respectability.

In *The Longest Journey*, the implication is made of man's connection, through earth, with the whole mysterious, ordered flux of the universe; yet the person who instinctively manages that connection, Stephen Wonham, is neither the major character nor of a type that gains Forster's central attention in any of the novels, and what sense we do gain of such an ordered flux actually proceeds less from Wonham's earth-relation than it does from the rhythmic imagery utilized by Forster (that imagery is discussed in the following chapter) and from the unsuccessful attempt of the protagonist, Rickie Elliot, to transfer to the sphere of human relations the stability of an absolute reality.

In *Howards End*, Forster gives the successfully achieved relation with earth not to the instinctive pagan but to a person who is closer to his own interests and sympathies. It is the intent of *Howards End* that Margaret Schlegel, through the assistance of Forster's own mythological creation, Ruth Wilcox, will attain from earth the means of achieving not only harmony within the realm of human relations, but also reconciliation between the physical and transcendent realms. *Howards End* marks the ultimate point which Forster reaches in his quest to find order through nature and earth, an order which gives meaning to the ceaseless change and seeming chaos of temporal existence. If one takes the four novels as a progression toward a goal, that goal is the reconciliation arrived at in *Howards End* between the world of human relationships and the world beyond; and the novel should hence stand as the fulfillment of its predecessors, the novel which gains the fullest measure of extension and prophecy, and to which *A Passage to India*, coming fourteen years later, would at best be anticlimactic.

Yet *A Passage to India*, which finds that earth can function no longer as a unifying element because man has become an alien upon its surface, and which does not give to the world of human relations any achieved harmony, not only gains a greater extension toward the universal regions than does *Howards End*, but attains what *Howards End* only, rather desperately, attempts —the pure prophetic utterance. The inference to be drawn is that achieved harmony, as expressed through Forster's nature and earth mythology, is actually foreign to the author's prophetic sense.

But it is rare in literature for any novel—indeed, one would be hard put to find a comparable example—to relate so closely to an author's intuitional, psychological, and mental positions as does *A Passage to India;* the themes of the earlier novels, regardless of their relation or lack of relation to Forster's ultimate sense of values, have imparted to these novels both durability and insight, and each of them is as "true" as the author can make it.

Fantasy: A Room with a View

Full understanding of Forster as novelist hence requires an understanding of all his novels, of his renunciation of themes as well as his development of them. For the earliest statement of those themes, one should turn to *A Room with a View*. Though it was published in 1908, only two years before *Howards End*, it was probably the earliest in conception, since Rose Macaulay tells us that the first half of a draft of *A Room with a View* was written in 1903; such a dating explains why the novel seems, in the spirit of fantasy which permeates it, the most obvious development from the early stories.

The artifice which marks the episodic sequence is in that spirit. The novel opens and concludes in the same pension in Florence, the pension where Lucy Honeychurch, the heroine, meets briefly the man she is later to marry, George Emerson. In the final chapter, she and George are united, and the return to the pension imparts the note of completion. But, in the interim, it is necessary to have complications develop at Lucy's home in Surrey, where she becomes engaged—through her own muddledom and self-deceit—to Cecil Vyse, a man for whom she has no love.

The story thus involves a triangle, but before it can be put in operation successfully, George Emerson must also put in an appearance at Surrey. This he does, having by chance encountered Cecil in the National Gallery; they are strangers, but Cecil coaxes him back into the story. And, since they too are necessary to the action, various other guests of the Florence pension reappear, murmuring polite apologies to the effect that they have come to this little corner of Surrey because the plumbing at home has broken down (Charlotte Bartlett, Lucy's chaperone in Italy); because of a transfer from one parish to another (the clergyman, Mr. Beebe: *he* prepared us for this move while we were still in Florence); because a bicycle tire went flat in front of the church (Lydia Lavish, the female novelist). And there are others too: the Miss Alans, sister spinsters, who float airily through Italy and England and thence into Greece, beckoning to Lucy with shy, bent fingers—dual fates of what she will become if she discards both Cecil and George.

Fruition and celibacy, the classical view and the medieval view, light and darkness, reality and hypocrisy —the first half of each of the four pairs opposes the latter half in contesting for the soul of Lucy Honeychurch. It is not a battle that suggests the suprahuman; none of the characters is, in the sense we have considered the word in the previous chapter, incomplete. Though they are not flat, they are far less intricate than the characters in any other of the novels, and when they will show us some new side of their personalities, it is apt to be through a single jackknife: Mr. Beebe, Cecil Vyse, and Charlotte Bartlett all perform for us in this manner. None of the characters, not even Lucy Honeychurch, suggests in any sense the psychological complexity that marks Rickie Elliot, that is implicit in Fielding and to a lesser degree in Philip Herriton, or the moral complexity of Margaret Schlegel. When Rose Macaulay comments that in this novel Forster "was pouring out his characters so lavishly and zestfully as if he had no future to save for," she was taken—as any reader might be—by the surface brilliance and the acrobatics which are a portion of the charm that fantasy may offer.

What gods and goddesses are involved? The Italian carriage driver who incenses Mr. Eager (a proponent of the second army) and who delights Mr. Emerson (the chief orator for the first) by his love-making on the excursion which is to result in the first kiss between George Emerson and Lucy—*he* is Phaethon, "a youth all irresponsibility and fire"; and Mr. Beebe, who straddles the fence between both forces, "recognized him at once." But the major, directing deities of one side are Eros and Pallas Athena; of the other, Erebus and his son Momus. The latter pair, unlike the former, are not mentioned by name, but strong internal evidence suggests their presence throughout: Momus, the god of scorn and mockery, operates through Cecil Vyse, the practical joker, in order to aid Erebus gain Lucy's soul.

Pallas Athena and Momus already have been involved in an earlier and more famous combat, that depicted by Swift in *The Battle of the Books;* parallels do exist, intentional or not, between that battle and the one which engages Forster's attention. The earlier struggle as well was fought over a view: the forces of Momus, representing the Moderns, occupied the smaller summit of Parnassus and were annoyed, Swift tell us, because the higher summit, "in quiet possession of certain tenants, called the Ancients . . . spoiled the prospect of theirs."

Like the Spider in *The Battle of the Books*, who lives within his castle of webs, "all built with my own hands, and the material extracted altogether out of my own person," Cecil Vyse is marked by a devastating self-sufficiency. From his remove—a remove which, in contrast to Fielding's, results from his sense of completeness—Cecil will offer advice, but neither really wants nor requires what others may be able to offer him. Of Cecil, Forster remarks that "he remained in the grip of a certain devil whom the modern world knows as self-consciousness, and whom the mediaeval, with dimmer vision, worshipped as asceticism." Because of that grip, Cecil is allied with the dark forces, the forces which are not only medieval but sterile; and so Mr. Beebe will remark that "Mr. Vyse is an ideal bachelor. . . . Like me, better detached."

As is equally true of *The Battle of the Books*, the opposing forces, those of light and fertility, are humanistic. The major humanist in Forster's novel is George Emerson's father, who tells Lucy, "We know that we come from the winds, and that we shall return to them; that all life is perhaps a knot, a tangle, a blemish in the eternal smoothness. But why should this make us unhappy? Let us rather love one another, and work and rejoice." Swift's humanistic spokesman is of course the Bee, and it is interesting to note the actual bee-motif of *A Room with a View*; for Forster, in the spirit of fantasy, has been playing with words. But one cannot, even if he should so wish, make of *The Battle of the Books* a tidy corresponding framework. Swift's satire seems somewhere in the background, but so is the Comic Spirit of George Meredith, and so too the personality and beliefs of Samuel Butler.[1] The main point to be made here is that Forster's novel, like *The Battle of the Books*, is essentially fantasy, and the fantastic approach accounts for its lightness of spirit, for the depiction of characters with such a bright splash of color and a single stroke of the brush, and for the gay disregard of probability.

The sense of reality which Lucy finally gains is a sense of physical reality only. She is brought to her perception of it through Italy, a land which in its people as well as its past is opposed to sham and convention; through the sight of human blood on some photographs she has bought at Florence in her pursuit of "Culture";

---

[1] In the essay, "A Book that Influenced Me," Forster indicates that *Erewhon*, "a serious book not written too seriously," influenced him most, because he found the ideas congenial, because it shows Butler as "a master of the oblique," and because it makes use of fantasy: "I like that idea of fantasy, of muddling up the actual and the impossible until the reader isn't sure which is which."

Lee Elbert Holt points out, in a *PMLA* essay, that during the time in which Forster was completing *A Room with a View* he was planning a never-finished critical study of Butler, and offers this as a possible explanation for the relationship between Butler and the elder Emerson. The latter's education of his son, one free of hate-inspiring religious superstition, is the kind which Ernest Pontifex gives his children in *The Way of All Flesh;* and Mr. Emerson's refusal to baptize George in his infancy relates to the quarrel which divided Butler from his family. Mr. Holt also finds that Mr. Emerson quotes from Butler's essay, "How to Make the Best of Life," when he says, " 'Life,' wrote a friend of mine, 'is a public performance on the violin, in which you must learn the instrument as you go along.' "—the thesis, also, of *The Way of All Flesh.*

and through a sequence of kisses with George Emerson, whose main function seems to be to pop up now and again like a jack-in-the-box to implant those kisses upon her. *A Room with a View* is Forster's only novel in which the vision doesn't reach outward, the only one in which the characters are "complete"; it is the novel of greatest artifice and improvisation, and the only one to end on an unreserved note of happiness—a celebration of joy in marriage and an expression of the harmony of life in accord with nature. It is, in other words, Forster's single novel written in the spirit of fantasy, and to it Forster's own description of what fantasy contains is generally appropriate:

The stuff of daily life will be tugged and strained in various directions, the earth will be given little tilts mischievous or pensive, spot lights will fall on objects that have no reason to anticipate or welcome them, and tragedy herself, though not excluded, will have a fortuitous air as if a word would disarm her.

Yet even in this novel, which so clearly invokes the deities of fantasy, one senses toward the conclusion a partial impatience on the part of the author with the limitations which fantasy imposes. Upon completing the early draft of the first half of the novel, Forster is quoted by Rose Macaulay as commenting, "My story distracts me. Clear and bright and well-constructed, but so thin"; and the latter portion of the published novel certainly reflects an attempt to give the novel a greater depth. It is a depth which does not belong to the province of fantasy: indeed, as the novel draws to a close, the gods and goddesses of fantasy seem to retreat out of sight, no match for the new force which has entered the story—the force of evil. That evil is the ultimate result of Lucy's refusal to see the physical reality, and it will vanish as soon as she comes to terms with that reality and behaves in accordance with nature; but the evil, with its accompanying sense of a darkness nearly absolute, is magnified to such an extent that it falsely gives the impression of having assumed an independent existence, an existence bearing no relation to physical reality at all.

Of *A Room with a View*, Rose Macaulay tells us that "in not liking it much, Mr. Forster was probably in a very small minority"; but the fact of his dissatisfaction is interesting, for it implies a dissatisfaction with fantasy itself and accounts for his continuing search for a mythology that would allow him a more adequate communication of his own particular values—values which have less to do with the play of the intellect than does the fantasy of *A Room with a View*, and more to do with the insights of intuition.

The Beginning of a Pattern: Where Angels Fear to Tread

Forster's first novel in publication sequence is *Where Angels Fear to Tread*; however, in the conceptual order it follows *A Room with a View*. If it is a more satisfying and successful novel than *A Room with a View*, the reason lies more in the fact that it is not written in the fantastic spirit of the other novel than it does

61

in any thematic differences; for the novel is concerned with the same basic issues. Philip Herriton has been substituted for Lucy Honeychurch as protagonist, and Philip must equally be made aware of the truth of the physical reality, of the truth of nature and earth. If the process toward awareness is painful for Lucy, we sense it only through the darkness settling over her, a darkness symbolic of the impending victory of one of the mythological forces; in *Where Angels Fear to Tread*, no arbitrary mythological referent is ever assumed, and attention centers more directly and with greater emphasis and power on the actual suffering—physical and psychological—which Philip Herriton must undergo before he is purged of all sham and adherence to suburban, middle-class English standards of convention and respectability.

A more complex figure than Lucy, Philip combines within his personality her major qualities with those of Cecil Vyse. For, like Lucy, he rather obscurely desires natural fulfillment, and he is prevented from achieving it by a weakness which makes him a pawn of others and a victim of all that is artificial within society; and, like Cecil, he assumes an attitude of self-sufficiency: he will not become engaged in "life"—he will remain at a remove from it and find its problems to be humorous and often absurd. More than Cecil's, Philip's self-sufficiency seems a pose and a protection; but in both cases, it relates to a basic *lack* in their personalities. For neither understands man's relation to natural forces; neither appears capable of sexual fulfillment. Philip is made aware of the power of nature when he, though only through passive acquiescence, violates its order through the theft of the offspring of another's fertility, the child of the Italian Gino. But Philip's awareness of nature, regardless of the extent to which that awareness brings purgation of all that is false within him, cannot, by the fact that physical love and reproduction are denied him, be accompanied by his identification with the natural forces; and the concluding pages of the novel offer him no hope of true completion and fulfillment.

Though the novel is not fantasy, neither can it be classified as prophecy; like *A Room with a View*, it does not extend beyond the physical reality, and though nature operates as a unifying force, it does so through no communicated sense of any authorial vision of universality. Rather, nature would seem to represent an ideal most clearly defined: whoever can be identified with nature is devoid of hypocrisy or sham. Though such an individual may be—as is Gino—brutal, he will remain honest; and to him is given the gift of fulfillment through fertility. If the novel aspires at all toward prophecy, it does so through the stress given that latter aspect of nature, its fertility; for the sense of a dark and powerful creative force is present in the Italian portions of the novel. Gino's brutality is seen, and justified, in relationship to such a conquering force; nothing can thwart the cyclical movement from creation, to death, to creation. Yet the deliberate manipulation of nature in the novel, its use as a framework around the action, hampers, as the next chapter more fully discusses, any extension it might bring. Neither prophetic nor fantastic, *Where Angels Fear to Tread* is more a subject for that following chapter than for this one; here it is of interest chiefly in that it marks the elementary stages of a pattern to be more extensively developed in the later novels.

For fruition and fertility are to remain central aspects of Forster's use of nature, and the fruition denied Philip Herriton is to be denied Rickie Elliot in *The Longest Journey* and Margaret Schlegel in *Howards End;* the sense one has of Philip's incompletion, though that incompletion is measured against the physical reality only, is similar to the incompletion characteristic not only of Rickie but of Fielding, the protagonist of *A Passage to India;* and Philip's detachment from the world of human relations constitutes a theme that haunts all of Forster's novels except *A Room with a View.*

The Divisions of Reality:
The Longest Journey

The two spheres of reality which Forster treats in his later novels are clearly apparent for the first time in *The Longest Journey.* Rickie Elliot, the protagonist, is conscious of a separation of reality into physical and transcendent realms; and, as a result, he is faced with a problem more complex than that faced by the protagonists in the short stories and in *A Room with a View* and *Where Angels Fear to Tread.* So far as these protagonists are concerned, reality has no divisions, no separation; their problem is simply to find "reality" and live in harmony with it.

Rickie's problem, on the contrary, is one of making a proper adjustment between the seen and unseen. On the one hand, he trusts implicitly in an incorruptible and divine reality; on the other, he is aware that life about him is without stability and that its values are far from absolute. Rickie suffers, we are told, "from the Primal Curse, which is not—as the Authorized Version suggests—the knowledge of good and evil, but the knowledge of good-and-evil." In part at least, Rickie typifies the religious problems of his age, an age which still holds to a supreme deity but which no longer can perceive His beneficent operation in the physical world. Rickie's crumbling commences when he perceives, with many of the Victorians after Darwin, not the goodness of nature, but rather a cruelty and chance which deny to mankind all sense of order. Aware of a frightening discrepancy between the world about him and the world of God, Rickie gives to the world about him the absolute values of the other. Such a distortion leads him, eventually, to disillusion and death.

The solution which the novel offers to such a problem as Rickie represents is simply a trust in the still-integrated reality which marks the instinctual life, the life which has been praised so extensively in the earlier novels. Hence one recognizes in *The Longest Journey* the presence of two mythological frames of reference: one which is Christian and involves, through Rickie, the present separation of physical from transcendent reality, and the other which is pagan and which finds its reality wholly within nature.

The Christian mythology is suggested through a parallel that exists between the Adam and Eve story and Rickie's own story. Both Genesis and *The Longest Journey* are concerned with the basic issue of man's double relationship with man and with divinity. It is interesting to note that three of the characters in the novel—Rickie; the girl whom he loves, Agnes Pembroke; and Rickie's aunt, Emily Failing—constitute a trio which, though never becoming an equivalent, continually reminds of the biblical trio of Adam, Eve, and Satan. Aunt Emily's mission is to refute all earthly and divine values which might lead to the attainment of human happiness, and it is she who, in the malice of such a mission, reveals the knowledge—under the central tree of the Cadbury Rings—that Stephen Wonham is Rickie's half brother. But if Aunt Emily is in any respect an embodiment of Satan, she is a Satan concerned with respectability: the secret of Stephen's parentage must be kept from Stephen himself, she believes, in order to prevent a family scandal from reaching the outside world. She readily wins Agnes into agreement, for she is wealthy and Agnes would not wish to be in her disfavor. Agnes, in spite of Rickie's initial opposition, persuades him also to withhold the information, even at the moment he goes to the window to answer a call from Stephen: "The girl darted in front of him. He thought he had never seen her so beautiful.

She was stopping his advance quite frankly, with wide-spread arms."

So Rickie makes the choice of Adam and sins in terms of the spirit. The choice becomes "like a poison we won't acknowledge"; and Agnes' voice, "which had lured him then ('For my sake,' she had whispered), pealed over him now in triumph." Like Adam, Rickie has disregarded the proper hierarchy. Forster comments, " 'if I had a girl, I'd keep her in line,' is not the remark of a fool nor a cad. Rickie had not kept his wife in line . . . and in consequence she was the worse woman after two years of marriage."

Rickie—it is a result of his Elliot blood, his failure in marriage, and his inability to sense the reality of earth—is not granted progeny; the girl-child born to him and Agnes is crippled even as Rickie himself and dies in infancy. Yet it is part of the novel's thematic trust in the flux and order of nature that when Rickie dies in saving a drunken Stephen from an oncoming train, he will gain a continuation through Stephen. Thus the novel ends on a note of optimism and a fore-telling of the future—a future in which Stephen's progeny will reign, the descendents, through Stephen, of Mrs. Elliot and her lover, Robert, and not those of the Elliot family, of which Mrs. Failing as well as Rickie is a member. It is through the pagan Stephen that salvation to mankind will be granted, and the deities who will grant it are Artemis and Demeter, twin goddesses of the Wiltshire countryside as well as of Greece.

67

And when, at the novel's end, Stephen views the Cadbury Rings, those mysterious tombs of long-vanished soldiers, and wonders "whose authority" has invested in him and his offspring the human destiny, his sense of unity and order springs out of the earth, and thus earth gives him fulfillment.

If, however, Forster does not quite meet the problem he has set up in this novel, the reason is that his own concern is with the task of reconciling physical with transcendent reality; and if such a reconciliation is, as he would seem to suggest, the problem which faces Rickie and contemporary society, then Stephen Wonham, whose chief virtue lies not in reconciliation at all but in an instinctive earth-acceptance, offers a solution which is much too simple. Indeed, in *The Longest Journey* Forster is too poignantly aware of the dual separation of man from man and of man from the transcendent reality to give complete plausibility to Wonham as a redemptive agent.

Such an integration as Wonham represents, involving as it does not only satisfactory human relationships, but the glorification of sexual power, is in contrast with the typical Forsterian remove from the world of human relationships, the position of detachment which is central to his use of point of view. If, in *The Longest Journey*, he departs again and again from that position to merge with Rickie Elliot, the most autobiographical of his characters, the identification with Rickie suggests less that Forster can successfully close the distance between himself and the world of active human relations than it suggests a partial explanation of his normal remove from it.

Moreover, as has already been noted in the introductory chapter, the descent of the point of view results in the empathetic merging not only of Forster but of the reader with Rickie and thus makes aesthetically unsatisfactory the epilogue's implication of Rickie's continuation through Wonham; for, desiring tragedy, we are granted hope. It is significant that in the two remaining novels the point of view remains consistently detached and that in neither of them does the instinctual pagan play a major role.

Prophecy and the Forsterian Voice

The matter of voice becomes more relevant in *Howards End* than it has been in the previous novels, for in *Howards End* Forster, though he does not achieve it, seems to be approaching a kind of prophetic utterance; it becomes even more relevant in *A Passage to India*, where he does achieve an effect pure enough to place him within that select group of writers Forster himself finds to be prophetic—Dostoevsky, Melville, Emily Brontë, and D. H. Lawrence. As an introduction to the last two novels, then, some fuller comment on the nature of Forster's own prophecy is required; and, in this respect, it is helpful initially to realize the limitations which circumscribe whatever prophetic achievements he does attain.

Assuredly one cannot claim for Forster the intensity of prophetic insight which he finds to be invested in

Dostoevsky, the writer who is mentioned first in Forster's discussion of prophecy in *Aspects of the Novel* and to whom he devotes the most illuminating of his remarks; perhaps such an insight may be obtained only by one who has suffered to an extent beyond the capacity of the ordinary individual, and though we have the sense of suffering and pain in Forster—who can read *The Longest Journey* or *A Passage to India* without discovering that fact?—it has been disciplined, restrained. Suffering is not the only element involved in prophecy; it is not so simple as that, or out of the carnage of every war would emerge a concerted chorus of prophetic song.

One reason that Forster seems less prophetic than Dostoevsky lies in the fact that in Dostoevsky, as in Melville, in Emily Brontë, and, one might add, in Shakespeare, the prophetic element is found largely *within* the character. The prophetic creation is, by and large, opposed to the western tendency toward democratization, toward leveling of the extreme in the fictional hero: it is in those creations which go far beyond the norm that the universality in Dostoevsky is found. In Forster, extension in the main comes from *without* the character, by means to be discussed in the following chapter; it results, inevitably, in a lessening of prophecy —at least a lessening in the merging of specific character with "infinity."

Another, and related, reason that Forster would seem a lesser prophet than Dostoevsky is Forster's greater ambivalence toward reason. Reason, one judges, is not trusted by either Dostoevsky or Forster; but whereas the distrust, accompanied by an emphasis on emotion, produces the psychological conflicts, the sudden changes and emotional outbursts in a Mitya or an Ivan, it has a much less pronounced effect on Forster's people. The difference might be quite simply explained in terms of nationalities, Russian and English; it is explained as well by the fact that in conjunction with Forster's distrust in reason is a distrust of absolutes, resulting in the paradox that the reasoning apparatus can, and must, be involved continuously in making choices, in selecting what is best from one scheme, what is best from another, in order to provide the greatest possible harmony within the temporal world. One senses in Forster a hesitancy to allow himself to be completely immersed; and immersion seems an aspect of the prophet, be he John the Baptist or Ahab. Forster will not hence be identified with any faith, code, or doctrine. "The human mind," he observes in *Aspects of the Novel*,

is not a dignified organ, and I do not see how we can exercise it sincerely except through eclecticism. And the only advice I would offer my fellow eclectics is: "Do not be proud of your inconsistency. It is a pity, it is a pity that we should be equipped like this. It is a pity that Man cannot be at the same time impressive and truthful."

It is the implication of such a comment in Forster's writings that causes Austin Warren to say that the novel form, more than the drama, is most compatible with such a person as Forster, for "the novel suits the mind which pushes beyond gossip and news but is unable or

71

unwilling to accept a creed. . . . Forster's essays, assembled in *Abinger Harvest* (1936), document the conclusion that he has ideas but no 'idea.' " The realistic writer may utilize as his nexus Marxism, anti-Marxism, glorification of a group, class, nation, or the like; but Forster will not be involved in the mistake of absolutizing any manifestation of the physical reality by making it his "idea," nor will he trust to a millennium, to any sudden conversion of humanity.

"Not by becoming better, but by ordering and distributing his native goodness," he remarks in his essay "What I Believe," "will Man shut up Force into its box, and so gain time to explore the universe and to set his mark upon it worthily." But upon such an insight, noble though one may feel it to be, no prophetic claim can be based, nor can it be made for Forster when he says, "The people I respect most behave as if they were immortal and as if society was eternal. Both assumptions are false: both of them must be accepted as true if we are to go on eating and working and loving, and are to keep open a few breathing holes for the human spirit." Again we may accept such a point of view, but not from the prophet; for a belief in the necessity of illusion can play no part in his utterance, else he becomes but a false idol whose lips are manipulated to make him murmur only what we desire him to say.

If we are to claim Forster as a prophetic voice, insistent or timorous, clearly we must look to something beyond this. His prophecy relates rather to what has been suggested in this and the earlier chapter, the sense of

separation which exists within the Forsterian cosmos.
Though the transcendent must perforce be operative on
the level of the physical reality, though there exists one
absolute unity which encompasses all divisions, all shat-
terings of the temporal world, still that absolute, so far
as the individual person is concerned, remains far above;
for the individual cannot approach the absolute through
reason, nor can he wholly comprehend it through intuition. Awareness of the separation between actual and
ideal is the curse, the blessed attribute, of the balanced
temperament, the temperament of the person who must
seek not integration but mediation; and it is here, in the
conscious separation between actual and ideal, that we
find the basis of the prophetic voice in Forster.

Dostoevsky's characters, Forster finds, convey to us
"the sensation of sinking into a translucent globe and
seeing our experience floating far above us on its surface, tiny, remote, yet ours." In Forster, the transcendental is implied, extension is gained, but not by our
"sinking" through the characters into it; rather, the
transcendental exists at all times as concept, and it is in
the relation between that transcendental unity and the
characters who are searching for a portion of it that we
find the extension to a region where they are "joined
by the rest of humanity." That region is one in which
infinitude may be glimpsed, but only at intervals at best;
it is a region haunted by incompleteness, by a people
who sense, however obscurely, their limitations—psychological, intellectual, spiritual—and yet in which culture, good will, and intelligence matter. Must matter,

for they provide what joys are available. Forster's is, then, a prophetic gift which arises from a compassionate, conscious awareness of the separation between character and transcendent verity, a separation which *ought* to be bridged, but which is not. The author's voice itself originates from a position between the human and transcendent realms, and its own detachment is comment on the theme of human incompletion and separation.

The Movement toward Prophecy:
Howards End

The means whereby the two realms can be, if not bridged, at least reconciled, remains the same in *Howards End* as in *The Longest Journey*. Yet though nature, through earth and place, still is the redemptive power, the person who achieves harmony is not the pagan. Instead, the person to whom such harmony is granted is Margaret Schlegel, a protagonist who contains within herself some of the major values which characterize the triumvirate of *The Longest Journey:* like Ansell, she is aware of the suprahuman reality which can never be fully comprehended by man; like Tony Failing, she trusts in human brotherhood; and, like Stephen Wonham, she finds in earth a unifying force. Hence, though the transcendent and physical realities for Margaret remain separate, the earth-relationship affords a sense of linkage between them.

Though there is no Stephen Wonham in *Howards*

End, the English countryside still may provide an opportunity for connection among men; in the farmhouse neighboring Howards End, Margaret Schlegel senses:

Here had lived an elder race, to which we look back with disquietude. The country which we visit at week-ends was really a home to it, and the graver sides of life, the deaths, the partings, the yearnings for love, have their deepest expression in the heart of the fields. All was not sadness. The sun was shining without. The thrush sang his two syllables on the budding guelder-rose. Some children were playing uproariously in heaps of golden straw. It was the presence of sadness at all that surprised Margaret, and ended by giving her a feeling of completeness. In these English farms, if anywhere, one might see life steadily and see it whole, group in one vision its transitoriness and its eternal youth, connect—connect without bitterness until all men are brothers.

It is an attitude not greatly different from that expressed in the short story "The Road from Colonus." Yet in *Howards End*, more than in the previous stories and novels, greater stress is laid upon the faculty of imagination, an integral element of the feminine spirit, as aiding the perception of unity gained through the earth. In this respect, Ernst Schlegel, Margaret and Helen's father, confutes his haughty Teutonic nephew by telling him:

Your Pan-Germanism is no more imaginative than is our Imperialism over here. It is the vice of a vulgar mind to be thrilled by bigness, to think that a thousand square miles are a thousand times more wonderful than one square mile, and that a million square miles are almost the same as heaven. That is not imagination. No, it kills it. . . . Oh, yes, you have learned men, who collect more facts than do the learned men of England. They collect facts, and facts, and empires of facts. But which of them will kindle the light within?

Imagination, "the light within," will enable Margaret Schlegel to make connection with her fellows through the help of nature, of the earth; and it will enable her to reconcile the seen and the unseen through "continuous excursions into either realm." Margaret Schlegel realizes that one "would not gain his soul until he had gained a little of the world," a concept which Rickie Elliot will not, cannot, maintain—possibly because he desires immediately to gain his soul and *all* the world.

Nature and imagination, then, constitute a base which offers Forster in this novel, as Wordsworth before him,[2] a sense of the connection between men and a belief in a spiritual reality. In the beauty and harmony of nature, one may sense a kinship with the past of the human race, and a kinship with one's own soul; but what if the kinship no longer is apparent? Margaret, in her reliance on nature, is in direct contrast with the society in which she lives, one without roots or apparent permanence in

[2] In *The Prelude*, Wordsworth, after commenting that the final development of his growth is the realization that the love of nature leads to the love of man, finds that it is not nature alone that achieves this development:

> "This spiritual love acts not nor can exist
> Without imagination, which, in truth,
> Is but another name for absolute power
> And clearest insight, amplitude of mind,
> And reason in her most exalted mood."

values, a cosmopolitan society which, in the instability of its urban environment, in its lack of ties to the earth which remains the source and nourishment of its people and to which they will inevitably return, has constructed in London a monstrous, ever-decaying and ever-rebuilt city to stand as "a caricature of infinity." That man may become a total alien to his natural environment is suggested as an imminent possibility near the conclusion of the novel, where we see London creeping out into the country, reaching toward Howards End itself. Such a possibility is countered only by Margaret's hope that "because a thing is going strong now, it need not go strong for ever. . . . This craze for motion has only set in during the last hundred years. It may be followed by a civilization that won't be a movement, because it will rest on the earth."

Margaret's hope is the hope of the novel, for it has been through Howards End and the unifying effect of the countryside that she has been able to achieve spiritual connection with the businessman Henry Wilcox. If, in *The Longest Journey*, the future is entrusted to Stephen Wonham, in *Howards End* that future—specifically, England's future—resides within such a connection as Margaret obtains: that of the inner life of imagination and contemplation to the outer life of action, the life which is responsible for the contemporary nomadic civilization. Obviously, then, though earth remains integral, what it as unifying agent offers Margaret Schlegel is not what it offered Stephen Wonham. *Howards End*, unlike *The Longest Journey*, attempts

77

to show the saving power of the earth-relationship for a person who more fully embodies the qualities which are in accordance with Forster's own sympathies—the individual who, more complex than the instinctual Pan, is educated, concerned with the problems of society, and gifted with both intellect and intuition—faculties which are united through the active play of the imagination.

To such a person as Margaret Schlegel, earth offers no such complete fulfillment as it imparts to Wonham. As is true of the majority of the Forsterian protagonists, fertility is not granted her; and, though the fertility of nature is once again stressed as part of the mysterious flux affording continuation to mankind, the mythological deity of nature in this novel, Ruth Wilcox, has, as we have seen, passed beyond fertility. And, though the novel's intent is otherwise, Margaret never gains the *active* participation within the realm of human relationships which we are told is Stephen's achievement. Indeed, neither Margaret nor Ruth Wilcox ever manages to convince in the manner both are thematically intended to convince, and the reason relates to the increased power of the Forsterian voice within the novel—a power which to a large extent results from its ability to maintain a consistent detachment. But its function as mediator in *Howards End* is paralleled by Margaret Schlegel, with the difference between voice and Margaret the difference of their respective positions —one above the human reality, the other immersed in it. Margaret will reconcile the human and transcendent realms so that she may live in harmony in the human; the voice senses the connection through its remove from both. Since it is the novel's thematic intent that Margaret will gain success in her attempt at mediation, that she will ultimately possess a measure of the insight which the Forsterian voice has always possessed, clearly some reconciliation must be made between the disparate positions of the two.

Such a reconciliation of Margaret and voice—in other words, of the positions of the human world and the detached mid-point—provides a major problem that Forster must solve in the novel: he dedicates himself to prove that what he knows to be true can be discovered amidst, and successfully applied to, the tangles of the human world. The difficulty is that the two positions can never quite be made to merge. Committed as Forster is to the world of human relationships, his greater commitment is to the region above—the point in the heavens where those human relations begin to fade before, or become resolved into, the brightening glow yet beyond.

Because, then, of the inevitable distinction between the two regions, Margaret verges toward the greater and more remote of the pair; and even though the reader is informed of the success of her mediation, he is left with the feeling that such a success, ironically, has made her more separate, more alone in the human world —the childless, compassionate nurse to human sufferings.

It is Ruth Wilcox, however, who most fully illustrates the inability of the two positions to merge, for she is supposed to be at the point where the two come together. As detached as voice, she understands the relative unimportance of people, and yet she is to be human herself, able to reconcile differences among other human beings. But she is the most significant failure of the novel. She becomes a *statement* of the transcendent unity, but neither a plausible human being nor a bearer of the true implications of voice. If *Howards End*, then, does not fully realize its prophetic potentialities, if an extension is gained but not to the degree that one might expect from a novel of truly heroic proportions, the reason is largely that the two commitments have been forced into closer partnership than Forster really can give them. The commitments have not been bridged in this novel, though the attempt has been made; Ruth Wilcox testifies both to attempt and to failure.

The Prophetic Novel: A Passage to India

This is not to say, of course, that by the time of *A Passage to India* Forster has been able to construct such a bridge. The last novel is his great novel, the one that most fully realizes its potentialities, and it does so partly at least because in it Forster is most keenly aware that the division does exist, that what he attempted without full success in *Howards End* is totally impossible now. Fielding has supplanted Margaret Schlegel as the protagonist who is concerned with the problem of human relationships; but earth no longer supplies a link between man and the transcendent unity. The voice remains, it can still remind of that unity, but without the aid of earth it cannot give to Fielding a sense of his own connection with it.

For the separation of man from earth and hence from ultimate reality which threatened in 1910 has become accomplished by 1924, a disaster which has had, for Forster as novelist, at least one brighter feature: it has meant that the two commitments which he could never quite reconcile have been divorced fully by forces not his own and that what has been perhaps his individual psychological inability has become the fault of an age; it has meant that Forster's own detachment from human reality has become the only means of sensing, however partially, the divine order. Fielding's achievements in the realm of personal relationships, inconclusive as those achievements finally become, are possible because he, as opposed to Margaret Schlegel, can "travel light"; he has no roots in society nor place and he desires none; he is associated with no sense of tradition.

Not that all the characters in the novel are completely without root. Aziz, we are told, "was rooted in society and Islam. He belonged to a tradition which bound him, and he had brought children into the world, the society of the future. Though he lived so vaguely in this flimsy bungalow, nevertheless he was placed, placed"; and it is because he is so placed, because he is aware of such a tradition, that, in spite of the brevity of his acquaintance with Mrs. Moore, the two make immediate and lasting connection. For she also is placed: she, like Aziz, has two sons and a daughter, and to her, "it is the

81

children who are the first consideration"; too, she is equally rooted by tradition—in her case, that of western Christianity.

But Aziz, though placed, "was without natural affection for the land of his birth" and must make a conscious, willful attempt to love it; and Mrs. Moore is in a countryside which is alien, even hostile, to her spirit. That is the difference that the years between *Howards End* and *A Passage to India* finally have forced upon Forster. India is more than a foreign land which the English may leave at their wish: it is the contemporary condition, the separation between all mankind and all earth. In her awareness of continuity and tradition, in her capacity for detachment and resignation, in the greatness of her encompassing love, Mrs. Moore is, indeed, Ruth Wilcox once more; but she is a Ruth Wilcox whose intuitive love remains after the major contributing factor to that love—a harmony between her spirit and the earth—has ceased to exist. Although she is fated to failure, we believe in her as we never believed, despite all of Forster's efforts, in Ruth Wilcox.

There is a paragraph in *Howards End* which stands as a foreshadowing of *A Passage to India* and will even do as a partial statement of the latter novel's intent. Marriage, we are told, "had not saved" Margaret

from the sense of flux. London was but a foretaste of this nomadic civilization which is altering human nature so profoundly, and throws upon personal relations a stress greater than they have ever borne before. Under cosmopolitanism, if it comes, we shall receive no help from the earth. Trees and meadows and mountains will only be a spectacle, and the binding force that they once exercised on character must be entrusted to Love alone. May Love be equal to the task!

In *A Passage to India*, no longer does man receive "help from the earth"; quite the opposite is true, for the earth even seems to increase the friction between men: "It was as if irritation exuded from the very soil. Could one have been so petty on a Scotch moor or an Italian alp? . . . . There seemed no reserve of tranquillity to draw upon in India. Either none, or else tranquillity swallowed up everything, as it appeared to do for Professor Godbole." The English Lake Country is referred to at various times in the novel, and it stands, in its contrast to the land around Chandrapore, as a symbol of the harmony that once existed between man and his surroundings; Wordsworth is in the background, Forster has acknowledged,[3] in the reference to Grasmere, whose "little lakes and mountains were beloved by them all. Romantic yet manageable, it sprang from a kindlier planet." But in India, beauty is lacking; Fielding "had forgotten the beauty of form among idol temples and lumpy hills; indeed, without form, how can there be beauty?" With the approach of the hot season, the sun returns "to his kingdom with power but without beauty—that was the sinister feature. If only there had been beauty! His cruelty would have been tolerable then."

[3] In a letter to the author of this study.

"May Love be equal to the task!" For Mrs. Moore, as we have seen, it is not: "God . . . is . . . love," He "has put us on earth to love our neighbours and to show it, and He is omnipresent, even in India, to see how we are succeeding," she tells Ronnie Heaslop. Yet God has not proved to be the satisfaction to her He was before her arrival in India: "She must needs pronounce his name frequently, as the greatest she knew, yet she had never found it less efficacious. Outside the arch there seemed always an arch, beyond the remotest echo a silence." And in the cave, in the unattractive, shapeless hills, she undergoes a psychic experience in which she loses totally the sense of values that her mystical divination of unity, related to the Christian tradition, has afforded her; she loses interest in Aziz, in her own children, in God. Yet Mrs. Moore has made a lasting effect, and she acts—*after* her negating vision, after her death —as an influence even more pervasive than that of Ruth Wilcox in *Howards End*. The Hindus at the trial of Aziz invoke her name in an echoing chant, for she has seemed like a goddess to them; she influences Adela toward realization that her accusation of Aziz has been false; her presence is felt throughout the final section of the novel and helps weave the achieved unity—transitory though it may be—that we find there.

In the important essay, "Art for Art's Sake," Forster, after commenting on the apparent impossibility of man's achievement of harmony "with his surroundings when he is constantly altering them," finds:

The future of our race is, in this direction, more unpleasant than we care to admit, and it has sometimes seemed to me that its best chance lies through apathy, uninventiveness, and inertia. . . . Universal exhaustion would certainly be a new experience. The human race has never undergone it, and is still too perky to admit that it may be coming and might result in a sprouting of new growth through the decay.

One sees in the depiction of Mrs. Moore a concept similar to this. She, who has always inclined toward resignation, must die through spiritual exhaustion—and this is achieved in the cave and not in her actual death on the sea—in order that a new birth, a new growth, may be achieved: the birth and growth which are portrayed for us in the final section of the novel. *Must* die—for the earth has become alien to man; the God, the order, the unity, which had been perceived through that earth must perforce be discovered again.

It is hence as a rebirth after exhaustion that we need to read the final section of *A Passage to India*. The novel's three sections represent, Forster tells us in his notes to the *Everyman* edition, the "three seasons of the Cold Weather, the Hot Weather, and the Rains, which divide the Indian year"; it is the recurring cycle of birth through death, commencing, in this novel, with the culmination of the period of fullest realization and maturity, proceeding thence through death to rebirth. The symbolic rites connected with the birth of Krishna, which relate to the Christmas observance in Christian tradition, even if they are primitive, even if they are muddled (perhaps partly *because* they are muddled), reach out in an attempt to encompass everything, to encompass the order which lies beyond chaos; and, because the ceremony is so all-inclusive, it prohibits anyone's discovery of "the emotional centre of it, any more than he could locate the heart of a cloud."

Obviously such a rebirth as this last section represents is one to be achieved neither through Christianity nor through the earth-relationship. Though one should not read the novel as a statement that Hinduism as such will solve the Indian dilemma, much less the dilemma of the world, Hindu metaphysics bears a number of definite relationships to the stabilized Forsterian philosophical position, a position which does not require place worship and which has always been hostile to organized Christianity. Certainly the redemptive power that Mrs. Moore possesses after death signifies chiefly in regard neither to place nor to her Christian religion; she becomes such a power, indeed, primarily only to the extent that she is merged with the small and elderly Hindu professor, Godbole.

Godbole, the central figure in the last section of the novel and the one most responsible for whatever sense of hope is granted there, is the only truly prophetic *character* in all the novels; for he is the only one who ever becomes the human counterpart of the Forsterian voice. To no locality on earth is Godbole indebted: he "always did possess the knack of slipping off," and he would be, one assumes, no less tranquil in London or even Chicago than he is in Chandrapore or Mau. For, like the voice, he is detached, though never to the extent of the full mystic. He remains, in his contact with human and transcendent realities, at precisely the midpoint of voice, and his is the same imperfect intuition: he is capable of comprehending the transcendent unity, but not completely. Thus, during the Krishna rites at Mau, he can love a wasp equally with a human figure recollected from his Chandrapore days—it happens to be that of Mrs. Moore—but he cannot equally love the stone on which the wasp rests: "no, he could not, he had been wrong to attempt the stone, logic and conscious effort had seduced, he came back to the strip of red carpet and discovered that he was dancing upon it."

Basic to the Mau ceremonies and to Godbole's desire "to attempt the stone" are the dual realities of Hindu metaphysics. Brahman is the unseen metaphysical absolute; the triad of Vishnu, Siva, and Brahma is the manifestation of Brahman. The metaphysical absolute is to be approached through the triad, but since Brahman is devoid of attributes, such an approach is, from the standpoint of logic, impossible. The triad, indeed, as is true of the phenomenal universe itself, offers a reality which is but illusory; hence identification with the absolute comes only with the extinction of individual consciousness, with the final and total separation of soul from the physical realm. One may love other existence within that realm in proportion to the extent of his own remove from the phenomenal universe; thus the detachment and self-abnegation of Godbole are qualities which impart to him his extensive, though necessarily incomplete, sense of love and unity—even as they have always been the qualities of the Forsterian voice, imparting much the same incomplete vision.

And so the rebirth suggested in the final pages of the novel is one to be brought about by a love which, in turn, can be obtained only through as great a denial of self and the physical world as it is possible for mankind to make. Is such a price too dear? Does the cost of the love make that love prohibitive? A recent critic of *A Passage to India*, Glen O. Allen, says that to Forster the Hindu Way of Love is a "good," although "not in its extreme nor to the exclusion of all other goods." The renunciation and loss of individuality which the Hindu must achieve in order to gain unity is, Allen believes, the "repugnant extreme"; and he feels that Forster in *A Passage to India* is asserting, as he did in *Howards End*, the need for proportion: love is but one of the "ingredients of the good life."

But such a proportion as Margaret Schlegel seeks between seen and unseen worlds in *Howards End* simply isn't a factor in this novel, for the seen world has become meaningless through man's own perversity and decay. The cost of love, to put it simply, has already been paid; man has already become the alien wanderer on earth's surface. Fielding and Godbole, those entirely different men, represent the division that exists between seen and unseen worlds; and they represent as well the disparity to be found between Forster's commitment to human relations and his commitment to the insight and love gained through a remove from those relations. No hope for a spiritual rebirth, for a new awareness of unity, can come from an emphasis upon the values of the human world; for, without the agency of earth, no valid sense of connection among men can be obtained. Fielding, despite his efforts in behalf of Aziz, still is denied brotherhood with him; thus those efforts, admirable though they may be, can produce no lessening of the spiritual sterility.

Harmony between man and nature may be gained at some time in the future, and perhaps once more there will be a reconciliation of seen and unseen worlds—we are given some slight indication of this by the landscape at Mau, which, while queer, is less alien than the rest of India; and we are granted some hope—it is, however, never stressed—in the as yet unborn child of Stella and Fielding. Stella, the daughter of Mrs. Moore, is her heir, so far as the possession of intuitive love is concerned; and hence Stella is also of spiritual kin to Godbole. Through the child of Stella and Fielding, mankind may once again achieve proportion and a balance between realms of reality. But, if so, the initiating power *must* come from a love which draws no sustenance either from nature or from human relations. Godbole and the Hindu Way of Love, absurd though they may seem to the western rationalist, can provide that power.

As is apparent by now, the major mythological referent of *A Passage to India* is that of Hinduism. Since the method whereby this referent is presented to us is primarily that of recurrent symbolism, the intricacies of the subject are best left to the following chapter on "Rhythm"; here what primarily needs to be noted is that such a referent has given Forster a framework totally in keeping with the implications of his voice and that the prophecy of the novel results from such a relationship.

A word of caution, however, is perhaps necessary. One can easily overemphasize the importance of Hinduism in *A Passage to India:* what we need to recognize, I think, is not that Forster accepts Hinduism, but rather that he selects from its metaphysics and attitudes those things which always have been most congenial to him. Reason, while important to Forster, has always been relegated by him to a position beneath that of love; and man's relationship to the physical world in *A Passage to India* is such that reason no longer can operate in conjunction with a spiritual insight. Other attitudes of Forster's which give him an affinity with Godbole have already been suggested. And clearly the Hindu division of realities—a division which, while affirming the existence of an absolute, makes its approach impossible to conscious man—offers a parallel to Forster's own philosophical view.

Toward the ceremonies of Hinduism, on the other hand, he shows little attraction. One assumes that Forster, with Stella and her brother, likes Hinduism while taking "no interest in its forms." Such an assumption is documented by *The Hill of Devi* (1953), an account of Forster's experiences in India in 1921 while he was serving as a personal secretary to the Maharajah of Dewas Senior. The description in *The Hill of Devi* of a Gokul Ashtami festival which he attended, and which provided him with the description of the Mau rites in *A Passage to India*, certainly indicates that the festival itself made no profound religious impression upon him. "There is no dignity, no taste, no form, and though I am dressed as a Hindu I shall never become one," he writes concerning his participation in the festival. What he chiefly responded to during the festival was the fact that it "touches something very deep in their hearts." [4]

Once we have discovered Forster's attitudes in *A Passage to India*, we can perceive the thematic progres-

[4] *The Hill of Devi* presents many of Forster's experiences which later were to be incorporated into *A Passage to India*: there is an account of an automobile accident which becomes the accident involving the Nawab Bahadur in the novel; there is a description of Mau (the Gokul Ashtami rites witnessed by Forster actually did not occur there); and there is always the sense of strangeness and lack of form in India. But *The Hill of Devi*, despite its wealth of background material, offers little new insight into the richness and depth of *A Passage to India*: for it is what Forster's creative faculty has done to the material which chiefly matters. In this respect, it is interesting to note in *The Hill of Devi* a comment on *A Passage to India*:
"I began this novel before my 1921 visit, and took out the opening chapters with me, with the intention of continuing them. But as soon as they were confronted with the country they purported to describe, they seemed to wilt and go dead and I could do nothing with them. I used to look at them of an evening in my room at Dewas, and felt only distaste and despair. The gap between India remembered and India experienced was too wide. When I got back to England the gap narrowed, and I was able to resume."

sion to be found in his novels, for it is a progression from a complete trust in physical reality to the denial of it in a Marabar cave, that cave, in its lack of attributes, representing the "nothingness" of the metaphysical absolute itself. It is a progression marked by Forster's choice of redemptive characters, from the elder Emerson to Gino, Wonham, Ruth Wilcox, and finally Godbole; and the disparity that separates the first from the last is, largely, the philosophical distance which Forster has covered within the relatively brief course of five novels.

Yet even the Forster who finds a parallel of his values in a Godbole and in Hindu metaphysics is not a writer who represents what we normally would consider the mystic state of being; he is, rather, a writer most keenly aware of discord and lack of harmony in his world who nevertheless senses, however obscurely, a harmony beyond and strives for identification with it. He never (or rarely) succeeds; it is difficult to determine whether or not Forster has ever attained the mystic vision, and Forster himself could never accurately tell us, as his account of the moment of birth during the Mau ceremonies indicates:

But the human spirit had tried by a desperate contortion to ravish the unknown, flinging down science and history in the struggle, yes, beauty herself. Did it succeed? Books written afterwards say "Yes." But how, if there is such an event, can it be remembered afterwards? How can it be expressed in anything but itself? Not only from the unbeliever are mysteries hid, but the adept himself cannot retain them. He may think, if he chooses, that he has been with God, but as soon as he thinks it, it becomes history, and falls under the rules of time.

And, in Forster's belief, if we lose a sense of unity with the earth, if we lose a sense of a divine plan in the stars, the loss, though profound, is ours only; it constitutes no denial of that ultimate order. For Forster's is a Shelleyian view, with the important exception that the veil cannot be fully penetrated to the absolute forms. All that Forster can do is suggest the presence of a transcendent verity. To do more is to absolutize what man cannot decipher; any absolute would be of man, not of the divine. Such a dissociation between man and ultimate truth is a basic distinction between Forster and the English Romantics and one reason that Forster's romanticism, idealism, can exist into the twentieth century while theirs cannot.

4 ∾

Rhythm

"Expansion. That is the idea the novelist must cling to. Not completion. Not rounding off but opening out. When the symphony is over we feel that the notes and tunes composing it have been liberated, they have found in the rhythm of the whole their individual freedom. Cannot the novel be like that?"

So asks Forster—the quotation was previously referred to in the introduction to this study—in *Aspects of the Novel*. It is hardly surprising that he, in trying to delineate what for him is a basic aspect of the novel, should turn to music for a parallel. In *A Room with a View*, we have felt his interest in music as Lucy Honeychurch begins to play the piano; and in *Howards End* there is that wonderful chapter describing the way various members of the Schlegel party react to Beethoven's Fifth Symphony at Queen's Hall: Aunt Juley, who taps out the tunes; Helen, who—like Forster himself, as we discover from an essay, "Not Listening to Music"—can dream up all sorts of accompanying images; Tibby, who concentrates on techniques, and so on. But it is Forster's address before the Harvard Symposium on Music in 1947 that constitutes his most emphatic declaration regarding music. He says that "music is the deepest of the arts and deep beneath the arts," that it, "more than the other arts, postulates a double existence. It exists in time, and also exists outside time, instantaneously." For the sequence of the parts fuses more completely with the whole in music than elsewhere: out of this fusion, he remarks in his discussion of rhythm in *Aspects of the Novel,* comes "a larger existence" than appears possible while we are engrossed in the sequence itself. And he comments that the writer may benefit from the example of the composer so that his work, likewise, may become an implication of something beyond, and greater than, anything within the work itself, an implication which can never be captured and interpreted successfully for us in terms of "message."

There are two major types of rhythm—that is, of "repetition plus variation"—available to the novelist, Forster says in *Aspects.* One is the "easy" rhythm, which, consisting of variations upon an image, corresponds to the musical phrase,[1] and which E. K. Brown

[1] For illustration of "easy" rhythm, Forster discusses, in a well-known passage of *Aspects of the Novel,* the use of the "little phrase" of Vinteuil's music in *Remembrance of Things Past.* For-

in a critical study of the novel form based upon Forster's concepts of rhythm, aptly calls the "expanding symbol." It has no regularity about it; indeed, Forster comments, "the function of rhythm in fiction" depends upon its fluidity, its refusal to follow a pre-established design: it is "not to be there all the time like a pattern, but by its lovely waxing and waning to fill us with surprise and freshness and hope." The development of "easy" rhythm comes spontaneously with the writing: something we presume is not quite so true of the other type, the "difficult" rhythm, which corresponds to the relation of the major "blocks of sound" in a symphony. "Is there," Forster asks,

any effect in novels comparable to the effect of the Fifth Symphony as a whole, where, when the orchestra stops, we hear something that has never actually been played? The opening movement, the andante, and the trio-scherzo-trio-finale-trio-finale that composes the third block, all enter the mind at once, and extend one another into a common entity. This common entity, this new thing, is the symphony as a whole, and it has been achieved mainly (though not entirely) by the relation between the three big blocks of sound which the orchestra has been playing.

Though Forster can find no analogy in fiction, Tolstoy's *War and Peace* affords the closest approximation, for "great chords begin to sound behind us" as we read, "and when we have finished does not every item—

ster's use of this kind of rhythmical device in *The Longest Journey* and, more extensively, in *Howards End*, precedes, of course, Proust's use.

even the catalogue of strategies—lead a larger existence than was possible at the time?"

This is the sum of what Forster has to say about both kinds of rhythm. His comments are brief but suggestive; they are of importance to the critic of Forster because Forster's own novels depend for much of their effect upon the use of rhythm. Indeed, Forster's use of musical devices is closely allied to his voice and to the prophetic utterance. To state it another way, music possesses a kind of *cumulative* effect for which the novel, though it deals with human beings and has none of music's unique laws, may strive: a cumulative effect resulting in a freedom and expansion not dissimilar to the freedom and extension of prophecy; for the whole matter of rhythm in the novel form is the prophetic faculty viewed, as well as one can view it, from a particular *technical* aspect.

A Room with a View *and* Where Angels Fear to Tread

The use of rhythm, as one might suspect, is much more pronounced in *The Longest Journey*, *Howards End*, and *A Passage to India* than it is in *A Room with a View* or *Where Angels Fear to Tread*; and, in the three novels which utilize it extensively, there is a progression in the extent of its use. The reason is clear enough: these are the three novels most concerned with the relation between the seen and unseen worlds, and in them we trace an increasing difficulty of man's perception of the transcendent reality. As the unseen retreats from man's awareness, the means to suggest its continued presence must be increasingly rhythmic, for the gap between the two worlds which the symbol connects becomes ever a wider gap, and the image must have in turn a wider and wider connotative value. A lump of clay, a mound of earth, can symbolize man's unity with man and universe in *The Longest Journey*, a wych-elm and a wisp of hay imply it in spite of all evidence to the contrary in *Howards End;* but in *A Passage to India*, the perception of that unity is normally beyond man's power: to him earth is primal and even malign; the visible world of clay and tree will not in themselves suggest a unity, for what he sees is apparently indicative of nothing beyond itself. Hence a richly developed rhythm of both "easy" and "difficult" varieties is required in the final novel to suggest the echoing spiritual vacuity *and* the order which still remains.

Rhythm is not a totally negligible factor, however, in *A Room with a View* and *Where Angels Fear to Tread*, though in neither novel does it often assume the proportions of an expanding symbol. When rhythm appears in these two novels, it usually does so as an aesthetic device or as an accompaniment to character and plot. Thus, in *A Room with a View*, the major images of light and darkness are to a large extent only tags to notify the reader which of the warring factions of the novel has gained dominance in the struggle for Lucy Honeychurch; and the violet, a representation of the flow of creation, appears in connection with whatever victories are attributed to the forces of light. It is on the hillside terrace of violets, the "well-head, the primal source whence beauty gushed out to water the earth," that George Emerson gives Lucy the first kiss. The frequent—perhaps too frequent—use of the image of the view relates to the forces of both light and darkness, for the view can be obscured or it can be what to the elder Emerson is the only perfect view: that "of the sky straight over our heads."

There is also the repetition of phrasing, a kind of rhythm to be noted in the later novels as well. Such a repetition—it is noted by Trilling in his study of Forster—is utilized to connect, in a peculiarly haunting way, the spinster Miss Catherine Alan with Lucy Honeychurch; for the aged spinster faintly reflects her own youth, and the young girl unwittingly accepts the barrenness of elderly spinsterhood. The reader is early informed of Miss Alan that "a delicate pathos perfumed her disconnected remarks, giving them unexpected beauty, just as in the decaying autumn woods there sometimes rise odours reminiscent of spring"; later, Lucy, having lost touch with youth through her hypocritical rejection of the man she really loves, is seized by some unaccountable emotion and becomes "aware of autumn. Summer was ending, and the evening brought her odours of decay, the more pathetic because they were reminiscent of spring."

Only one recurrent image of the novel ever seems to take on some of the qualities of an expanding symbol. It is the symbol of water, which, though used with less intricacy, reminds one of the water imagery of *The Longest Journey*, and its even more complex use in *Howards End*. Water is always in the background in *A Room with a View*, a suggestion of unity and the creative force as Lucy obstinately pursues her solitary way into darkness. The autumnal rains—those rains which constitute a major concluding image not only in this novel but in *Where Angels Fear to Tread* and *A Passage to India*—mark the ending of a cycle with the promise of a new one; like love itself, rain and river and sea manifest the miracle of continuation which exists within change. Thus the darkness begins to retreat from Lucy when she realizes the truth of old Mr. Emerson's words: " 'You love George!' And after his long preamble, the three words burst against Lucy like waves from the open sea."

The Arno River forms a kind of frame for the novel, taking on an added significance with each reappearance. It is mentioned in the introductory pages, and the climactic moment of the first part occurs on an embankment of the river. The moment is precipitated by the sudden murder of an Italian near the fountain in the Piazza Signoria, a murder which Lucy sees; she faints into the arms of George Emerson, who has also been a bystander. It is not so much the physical violence itself that affects them both. It is the stream of blood—flowing from the dying man's mouth and spotting the photographs Lucy has just purchased in her pursuit of culture rather than of life—which shocks George as well as Lucy into reality. The blood has made them

aware of a reality before which all that is artificial fades;
moments afterward, Lucy, "leaning her elbows on the
parapet . . . contemplated the River Arno, whose
roar was suggesting some unexpected melody to her
ears." In a brief last chapter, which brings the season of
spring back into the novel, George and Lucy, married,
stand by a window in the same pension in Florence
where they first had met. They are serenaded by a carriage driver who "might be that very Phaethon who
had set this happiness in motion twelve months ago";
his song "announced passion requited, love attained. But
they were conscious of a love more mysterious than
this. The song died away; they heard the river, bearing
down the snows of winter into the Mediterranean."

It is neatly done, this use of water imagery; but it
seems *too* neatly done to achieve any extensive expansion—the rhythm has primarily served the plot and ties
together all the action into a unified whole. And much
the same comment applies to the recurrent imagery of
Where Angels Fear to Tread. In this novel, two images
impart a major effect: the towers of Monteriano and the
dark wood with its sea of violets which is found along-
side the road that approaches the town. The former relates to the Dark Ages—for Monteriano is one of the
remaining bastions of that period—and the latter not to
the pastoral beauties but to the vitality, the almost ter-
rifying elemental beauty, "the terrible and mysterious"
nature of the Italian countryside. There is the suggestion of unreality in both town and countryside—an
unreality, that is, to the foreigners, who are forced to

THE NOVELS OF E. M. FORSTER

contend with an environment against which their train-
ing and their English suburban culture has afforded no
defense. All that is sham in them will topple; they will
be rejuvenated or destroyed.

Not that the towers represent a "right" view. They
are symbolic of human potentiality in either direction:
if they represent an admirable simplicity of elemental
passion, they represent as well darkness and confused
violence and stand for a kind of degradation and
falsity. Philip, observing one of them from his hotel
window, comments, "It reaches up to heaven . . . and
down to the other place." At the moment, "the summit
of the tower was radiant in the sun, while its base was in
shadow and pasted over with advertisements," and
Philip asks, "Is it to be a symbol of the town?" Here is a
less complex, a more blunt, use of imagery than we find
in Forster's later novels, a criticism one might make as
well when, just before the ill-fated kidnaping of Gino's
baby, Philip can only see of the same great tower "the
base, fresh papered with the advertisements of quacks."
The tower of the Collegiate Church of Santa Deodata
serves much more adroitly: Forster proceeds from the
tower to a description of the saint herself, a description
which is not only a beautifully ironic commentary but
which develops a minor variation upon the major theme
of Philip's refusal to accept responsibility in his world.
His supercilious detachment in the name of culture corresponds to the religious detachment of Santa Deodata,
who

was a holy maiden of the Dark Ages, the city's patron saint, and sweetness and barbarity mingle strangely in her story. So holy was she that all her life she lay upon her back in the house of her mother, refusing to eat, refusing to play, refusing to work. The devil, envious of such sanctity, tempted her in various ways. He dangled grapes above her, he showed her fascinating toys, he pushed soft pillows beneath her aching head. When all proved vain he tripped up the mother and flung her downstairs before her very eyes. But so holy was the saint that she never picked her mother up, but lay upon her back through all, and thus assured her throne in Paradise. She was only fifteen when she died, which shows how much is within the reach of any school-girl.

The little wood appears but briefly in the novel: we see it with Philip for the first time as he approaches Monteriano on his errand to rescue Lilia from her Italian lover; we see it again near the novel's conclusion, and this time it is the location where the carriage overturns, spilling the occupants to the ground and resulting in the death of Gino's baby. This is the extent to which the wood is utilized; yet somehow, even though its use is not in all respects successful, it is one of the lasting impressions we carry away with us after we have closed the cover of the book.

For the recurrent image here has, among other things, imparted a unity to the novel. The effect of the initial view is one of the unlimited creative strength of the violets; yet their luxuriant fertility, going far beyond mere beauty, is in contrast with the foreboding wood itself, with its "small and leafless" trees. It is early spring, the transitory moment when one can see the full cycle of nature, so that promise and threat become one. It is indeed from that basic creative intent of nature, the irresistible drive toward continuation beyond death, that Philip's detachment—as was noted in the previous chapter—is at least partially a refuge. The Herritons as a family group represent Sawston respectability (even Philip in his cynicism is a victim of it), with its submission to convention and hypocrisy: their withdrawal from basic truths has made them so "sterile" that the theft of a baby, offspring of Mrs. Herriton's daughter-in-law and an Italian primitive, is highly fitting. As we read of the trees whose "stems stood in violets as rocks stand in the summer sea," of the cart ruts turned into "hollow lagoons" by the violets, of the margin of the road as "a causeway soon to be submerged under the advancing tide of spring," do we not think back a few pages to the conclusion of the previous chapter, where we left Mrs. Herriton in her garden, having discovered the sparrows had stolen every one of the peas in the furrows—because she, thrown into her futile counter-offensive by the news of Lilia's engagement, has forgotten to rake the peas under the earth?

At any rate, the effect of the violets and the wood is not lost on Philip on this initial journey to "save" Lilia, for "his eyes had registered the beauty, and next March he did not forget that the road to Monteriano must traverse innumerable flowers." It is the hint we require that Philip is capable of salvation, capable still of response to real "life": the salvation that finally comes,

most appropriately, within the same wood. Yet it is not
next March, but in August of a later year that the wood
returns to the story. It is without flowers now; the trees
are dark, even darker than normal, because the carriage
carrying Harriet, Philip and the abducted baby enters
it in the midst of a torrential storm, the rain of a summer's end which replaces the tidal flow of spring. The
carriage overturns; the outcome, we know, would have
been tragic regardless, for Harriet's action has been a
tragic and stupid blunder.[2]

What takes place is precisely that which was implied
by the earlier image: out of death comes rebirth; it is
Philip Herriton who is "born" from the death of the
baby. The cycle emerges triumphant, much as it does
in *A Passage to India;* one almost inevitably tends to
refer forward to Forster's last novel when thinking of
this one. Fielding is an older, a wiser and sadder Philip
Herriton; both are "lost" men for whom some redemp-
tion is possible, since an ordered cycle does exist beyond
their awareness. For Fielding, it is not to be found in
nature, on this earth; for Philip, it is. The difference lies
here, and it forces Forster into greatness in the later
novel, into the farther-reaching, more beautifully developed rhythmic techniques of *A Passage to India.*

How else account for the differences in two novels

[2] In spite of this, the accident imparts to us, on the level of
purely physical action, an uncomfortable sense of a *deus ex machina* at work, a feeling not at all obliterated by our realization
that it doesn't bother Forster whether it is a *deus ex machina* or
not.

which possess other, even more striking, similarities? The final relationship of Philip and Caroline is not far removed from that of Fielding and Stella, in spite of the marriage of the latter pair. The accident in the wood is paralleled by the concluding section of *A Passage to India*, for in both one finds a heavy seasonal storm accompanied by the culmination of a story developed in close relation with the seasons themselves; in both a death (baby and rajah) is accompanied by a sense of rebirth; and in both there is at least the partial realization of unity following an immersion: Philip is tumbled into the water and mud where the violets grew, a baptism followed by the torture which is his purgation, and the boats of Fielding and Aziz collide and capsize in the flooded Mau tank during the Krishna rites.

The parallels suggest that, thematically, *Where Angels Fear to Tread* is far from slight, despite pleasant exuberances and a social satire reminiscent of theater comedy; its lack of complexity, in comparison with *A Passage to India*, is in its development of fewer variations in imagery, in less of a rhythmic "reaching out." For the success of the little wood, with its two brief appearances, is, like the River Arno in *A Room with a View*, more in the province of the final order it brings to the novel's form than it is in anything else. What one finds in the novel is what Forster will emphasize throughout all the novels: the continuation which exists within change, the real which coexists with the actual; but it is not until the real begins to rise farther from the earth, until the complete perception of it is no longer to be achieved through physical reality alone, that prophecy through voice and rhythm soars the reader into the unknown: for prophecy, as we find it in Forster, requires us to enter the regions where total self-fulfillment is never achieved.

The Longest Journey

The inconstant, unsubstantial state of man's affairs is stressed from the time of *The Longest Journey:* one of the recurrent motifs of the novel is that of the fragility of human existence, the fact that "we are all of us bubbles on an extremely rough sea." The numerous deaths, including Rickie's own, all of which are disclosed with such calmness and brevity, are a part of this view. Over the door of Rickie's Cambridge rooms "was his name, and through the paint, like a grey ghost, he could read the name of his predecessor."

In the face of such seeming human transitoriness and fragility, man is seen by Forster to have established monuments of immobility, rigid images in the time flux; and they are those in which Rickie, to his own destruction, will place his trust. In this category is to be placed the institution of Christianity; thus the Roman Catholic church at Cambridge "watches over the apostate city, taller by many a yard than anything within, and asserting, however wildly, that here is eternity, stability, and bubbles unbreakable upon a windless sea." Regardless of denomination, whether Roman or Anglo-Catholic, Christianity bears connection with another aspect of contemporary civilization, Sawston School; and Herbert Pembroke, teacher and clergyman, represents both. For the school, like the church, signifies chiefly as an institution, toward which all members must present a single, unified appearance. "Organize." "Systematize." "Fill up every moment," "Induce *esprit de corps*"— these are the watchwords of Sawston, and "they ignored personal contest, personal truces, personal love. By following them Sawston School had lost its quiet usefulness and become a frothy sea, wherein plunged Dunwood House, that unnecessary ship."

The pursuit of such uniformity and stability, goals to be gained only through the arbitrary absolutizing of an institution, leads them only to deception and chaos; in terms of religion, it has made the church a symbol remote from individual man and his relation with earth. In the burial mound of the Cadbury Rings, that symbol which represents past confirmation of man by earth, the cracked Cadover church bell, to whose sound Rickie is ultimately buried, becomes "petty and ludicrous." If the Salisbury cathedral spire never becomes a similar symbol of the inadequacy of the religious institution, the reason is that it maintains, like the pagan mound of the Rings, a kind of unresolved mystery, and stands, though it is of a later period, as a kind of past confirmation by earth. Stephen finds that his heart leaps up at the sight of the spire; it does so because for him, in spite of his disavowal of Christianity, it is part of the earth still, part of the Wiltshire region he loves. Spire and Rings are brought together for us in the final section of the novel by the essay of Tony Failing which Rickie reads: "Let us love one another. . . . It is all that we can do. Perhaps the earth will neglect our love. Perhaps she will confirm it, and suffer some rallying-point, spire, mound, for the new generations to cherish."

Tony Failing himself represents another kind of stability in which mankind, and Rickie, will trust: the images of the dead. Voices of the dead—of Tony Failing, of Robert, and, most important, of Rickie's mother —whisper through the novel, offering visions of love and truth. Thus it is that Rickie will leave Agnes to go with Stephen because in Stephen's urging he hears another voice, that of his mother, telling him to come. "Habits and sex may change with the new generation, features may alter with the play of a private passion, but a voice is apart from these. It lies nearer to the racial essence and perhaps to the divine; it can, at all events, overleap one grave." Yet a face from the dead, "however beloved, was mortal, and as liable as the soul herself to err." Man errs, indeed, when out of a spiritual craving for permanence he immobilizes any image; for from such immobility comes not permanence and order but only an illusion of them. So it is that against the frozen images before which Rickie will worship are contrasted those images which are of the natural flux, of the mysterious flow which imparts continuation to all existence within the phenomenal universe and with which man's "bubble" will finally unite.

Water—stream and sea—suggests throughout such a flux; and, as has already been indicated, so does that major image of the Cadbury Rings. The Rings, Forster comments, "were curious rather than impressive. Neither embankment was over twelve feet high, and the grass on them had not the exquisite green of Old Sarum, but was grey and wiry. But Nature (if she arranges anything) had arranged that from them, at all events, there should be a view." That view, indeed, is one of the whole system of England. "Here," says Forster, "is the heart of our island: the Chilterns, the North Downs, the South Downs radiate hence. The fibres of England unite in Wiltshire, and did we condescend to worship her, here we should erect our national shrine." That the Rings, graves of the ancient dead that they are, represent, through man's relation with the past, a basic truth, one knows from the parallel that exists between their geometric pattern and one which Ansell draws to illustrate reality for Rickie: reality, says Ansell, exists in the center of the circles and squares: it is "the one in the middle of everything, that there's never room enough to draw." For the Rings are described in a somewhat similar fashion: "A bank of grass enclosed a ring of turnips, which enclosed a second bank of grass, which enclosed more turnips, and in the middle of the pattern grew one small tree. British? Roman? Saxon? Danish? The competent reader will decide." It is beneath the central tree of the Rings that a major symbolic moment of the novel ensues, for there Rickie learns from a vindictive Mrs. Failing that Stephen Wonham, her sheepherder, is his half brother: this is the relationship which the past has bequeathed to him, and this is the relationship which he, through Agnes' intervention, will deny to the defeat of his own happiness on earth.

A symbol which, though it appears less frequently than the Rings, achieves an even greater expansion is that of the constellation of Orion. The reader sees it for the first time against that insistent motif of change and temporality in human existence. Rickie is becoming isolated from his wife, and his child has just died; he perceives more strongly than ever "the cruelty of Nature, to whom our refinement and piety are but as bubbles, hurrying downwards on the turbid waters. They break, and the stream continues." Rickie, aware then of the continuation, sees it arbitrarily given, however, to his half brother and not to him; in his desperation, he prays hysterically, and awakens from a dream in which his mother has comforted him:

He heard his mother crying. She was crying quite distinctly in the darkened room. He whispered, "Never mind, my darling, never mind," and a voice echoed, "Never mind—come away—let them die out—let them die out." He lit a candle, and the room was empty. Then, hurrying to the window, he saw above mean houses the frosty glories of Orion.

In Forster's short story, "The Point of It," Micky, being harrowed in the shapeless sands of Hell, remarks to another voice, "It would be appalling, would it not, to see Orion again, the central star of whose sword is not a star but a nebula, the golden seed of worlds to be"; and, in *The Longest Journey*, Orion, the constellation of autumn, is associated as well by Rickie with the promise of rebirth and continuation. When he senses in himself a kind of spiritual rebirth—aided materially by his new-gained knowledge that his half brother is his mother's son, not his father's—and at long last accepts Stephen as his brother and the one to whom continuation will be granted, he comes to realize the implication of the earlier dream and "hurried to the window—to remember, with a smile, that Orion is not among the stars of June."

But Rickie is doomed to affix all stars in position: Orion becomes finally to him as frozen an image as does his mother, and through his mother, Stephen; and when Stephen refuses to remain a "fixed" image, all collapses. Gone is all awareness of continuity, all hope for confirmation; the stream—that central flux symbol—no longer has meaning, "though it burst from the pure turf and ran for ever to the sea. The bather,[3] the shoulders of Orion—they all meant nothing, and were going nowhere."

One thinks, when reading of Rickie's spiritual disintegration, not only of a kind of paralyzed imagery of church and dead, but back to Rickie's secluded dell near Madingley. The dell, like the other images in flux, will

---

[3] A memorable event in the novel, and one which just precedes the disaster, occurs when Stephen and Rickie, in a carriage on their way to Rickie's final meeting with Mrs. Failing, stop by a stream to let their horse drink. Stephen bathes; but before this takes place, he lights a paper and puts it in the water: it is symbolic of the consuming but ever-burning life flame in the ceaseless flow.

appear impervious to time; and it is that seeming imperviousness which gives to it a peculiar charm. The dell "could not have been worth a visit twenty years ago, for then it was only a scar of chalk, and it is not worth a visit at the present day, for the trees have grown too thick and choked it"—but when Rickie loved it, the dell was for a brief moment secluded even from time: "The chalk walls barred out the seasons, and the fir-trees did not seem to feel their passage." The reader is told twice of the timeless appearance of the dell, and to each description is appended a brief contrast, each noting the passage of a different season. "Only from time to time would a beech leaf flutter in from the woods above, to comment on the waning year, and the warmth and radiance of the sun would vanish behind a passing cloud," we are informed in the earlier contrast; and it is echoed in the later, which occurs as Agnes acknowledges her love for Rickie: "Only from time to time the odours of summer slipped in from the wood above, to comment on the waxing year." Are these "comments" a threat or a promise? It could be the latter; to Rickie, it must finally be the former, for his quest of stability is such that it inevitably results in a refusal to acknowledge the continuity which he himself has at least partially recognized to be a manifestation of the divine order.

Chalk—such as that which surrounds the dell—reappears strongly as image in the final section of the novel. It is a recurrent token of the purity, of the vitality of earth, of the power which earth has over conventions; Stephen has the habit of lobbing pieces of it through windows. A more artful use of this imagery is in the scene in which a lump of chalk falls from Rickie's hand and shatters one of Mrs. Failing's teacups. The accident immediately follows Rickie's momentary triumph over Mrs. Failing and, through a delicately achieved sense of foreboding, hints at the disaster to follow. The incident has an additional implication: the chalk represents Rickie's method of salvation, and its destruction of the teacup—one of a prized harlequin set—suggests its power over Mrs. Failing's contrived idiosyncrasies and artificiality. But no such salvation is to be granted Rickie: the incident, seemingly so trivial, has been heightened into a significance which almost instantly vanishes; Leighton, the servant, asks that Rickie explain to Mrs. Failing what has happened, and he agrees. That the moment, however, *has* been significant, and that it represents an essential failure for Rickie, we know from its relation to an early comment Forster has made about Rickie and his Cambridge friends, who

have not tasted the cup—let us call it the teacup—of experience, which has made men of Mr. Pembroke's type what they are. Oh, that teacup! To be taken at prayers, at friendship, at love, till we are quite sane, efficient, quite experienced, and quite useless to God or man. We must drink it, or we shall die. But we need not drink it always. Here is our problem and our salvation. There comes a moment—God knows when—at which we can say, "I will experience no longer. I will create. I will be an experience." But to do this we must be both acute and heroic. For it is not easy, after accepting six cups of tea, to throw the seventh in the face of the hostess. And to Rickie this moment has not, as yet, been offered.

That moment, near the novel's end, has finally been offered him; through suffering, through experience, Rickie has arrived at a clearness of insight which enables him to see that Mrs. Failing has deceived herself, while he, on the contrary, "stood behind things at last, and knew that conventions are not majestic, and that they will not claim us in the end." It is at precisely this instant that the chalk breaks the cup; but with Rickie's ensuing promise of an apology, it is clear that his opportunity for salvation is lost and his final disaster will soon follow.

Any discussion of the rhythmic imagery of *The Longest Journey* would be incomplete without a reference to the Roman road level crossing, which, with Orion and the Rings, constitutes the most satisfying imagery in the novel. Structurally, it has an even more important function than the other two: it performs much as does the little wood with its sea of violets in *Where Angels Fear to Tread*, for it serves in one aspect as servant of plot to bind the novel together. As a device, however, the level crossing is the much more intricate image, a motif that appears in the initial part and that intrudes and fades continually throughout the middle and final sections. It carries with it the theme of the "bubble," of man's fragile existence; for each recurrence reminds us that here a child died, run over by the train bringing Rickie and Agnes to Cadover. Rickie will not believe the tragedy: he cannot grasp, this early and admirably contrived reference indicates, that death and love can be in such juxtaposition; for at the moment of the catastrophe he has been holding his loved one in his arms. The crossing is on Mrs. Failing's property, and Stephen, soon after the arrival of Rickie and Agnes, becomes angered by Aunt Emily's endless mockery, her indifference to the danger of the crossing: " 'There wants a bridge,' he exploded. 'A bridge instead of all this rotten talk and the level-crossing.' "

It is at the same crossing that Rickie's final, weary awareness of love brings his death as he rescues the drunken Stephen, only to die himself. In the epilogue, the reader is informed that a bridge has finally been constructed; and, in the concluding paragraph, night has fallen, and the whistle of a train—it is carrying Herbert Pembroke from his meeting with Stephen—"came faintly, and a lurid spot passed over the land—passed, and the silence returned." What has been imparted, as Peter Burra and many other readers have noted, is an extraordinary "sense of completion"; but it is, even more than a completion, the reconciliation of opposing themes. For the building of a bridge at the Roman road crossing is more than the spanning of a railroad track: it is the spanning of the temporal in existence, the implication that the past and the continuity which is of the earth—all that, in other words, which has been represented by the dead, the Cadbury Rings, and the Roman road itself—need not be severed by the inevitable movement of time, by the train on its iron track, which is at once symbol of another change, that of man's technological advancement. The bridge and train are comment on that which Rickie has never wholly grasped: the coexistence of unity with mutability.

Howards End

Although from the standpoint of publication dates *A Room with a View* (1908) comes between *The Longest Journey* (1907) and *Howards End* (1910), it apparently is, as has been indicated, Forster's earliest novel from the standpoint of conception. But, irrespective of dates, *The Longest Journey* and *Howards End* are more complex works both structurally and thematically, and bear certain relationships.[4] The theme of instability and change remains in *Howards End* as a dominant aspect, but, although two sudden deaths occur —those of Ruth Wilcox and Leonard Bast—primary emphasis is not given to the concept of life as a "bubble." Human relations must stand up under a greater burden than they have known in the past, Forster remarks in *Howards End;* for man is creating, through his increasing cosmopolitanism, a "nomadic civilization" through which he "shall receive no help from the

[4] One of these relationships, the parallel between Rickie Elliot and Helen Schlegel, has been commented upon in the chapter on "People."

earth." Yet "help from the earth" still is a hope of the novel, although the ending—with the tides of London creeping nearer and nearer Howards End—is far from a statement of full optimism.

What kind of help may the earth still offer? "Of Pan and the elemental forces," Forster says in the novel, "the public has heard a little too much—they seem Victorian, while London is Georgian—and those who care for the earth with sincerity may wait long ere the pendulum swings back to her again." And Forster himself has moved away from Pan in *Howards End:* we find no equivalent of Stephen Wonham in this novel.[5] There still remains, however, hope for an awakening to the continuity and unity which the earth affords. The Cadbury Rings, one of the symbols of this in *The Longest Journey*, is now replaced by Howards End, its hayfield, wych-elm, vine, and garden, and by the neighboring Six Hills. The latter we meet for the first time when Aunt Juley journeys from London to Howards End to meddle in Helen's already-terminated love affair with Paul Wilcox, and reference is made to them

[5] In spite of the movement away from the Pan character in Forster, *Howards End* still finds hope in the men whose hours are ruled, "not by a London office, but by the movements of the crops and the sun. That they were men of the finest type only the sentimentalist can declare. But they kept to the life of daylight. . . . Half clodhopper, half board-school prig, they can still throw back to a nobler stock, and breed yeomen." Hope for the future in *Howards End* resides in the child of Leonard Bast and Helen Schlegel, and Leonard is of "the third generation, grandson to the shepherd or ploughboy whom civilization has sucked into the town."

throughout the novel. But the Six Hills, "tombs of warriors, breasts of the spring," make their greatest implication as the novel draws to its climax, for within sight of them comes the crisis of Margaret and Henry's relationship, when Henry refuses to "connect," refuses Margaret's request to allow Helen to remain overnight at Howards End. For Margaret, it is a moment, curiously, of victory as well as defeat. The defeat is obvious: she realizes that "there was nothing more to be done," that their love has gone over the precipice, "but perhaps the fall was inevitable." The victory comes through the resignation which accompanies her awareness of failure and which is her final movement toward spiritual kinship with the first Mrs. Wilcox: "At such moments," says Forster, commenting upon Margaret's attitude as she realizes the failure of the marriage, "the soul retires within, to float upon the bosom of a deeper stream, and has communion with the dead, and sees the world's glory not diminished, but different in kind to what she has supposed. She alters her focus until trivial things are blurred."

Before the novel can end on any note of optimism, a sense of failure, followed by new spiritual insight, must also occur within Henry.[6] And so it does, now on a grassy incline of the Six Hills. Margaret, preparing to leave Henry forever, hears from him that his son

[6] Realization of failure, accompanied by resignation in varying degrees, comes to all the major characters, Leonard Bast and Helen as well as Margaret and Henry. It is, indeed, the sense of resignation which gives to the conclusion a profound depth of sadness in spite of Margaret's achievement.

Charles is to be indicted for manslaughter in connection with the death of Leonard Bast, an indictment which, as Henry himself realizes, involves Henry's own "breaking." It is, for him, the death of all that in the past has denied him connection. "Margaret drove her fingers through the grass. The hill beneath her moved as if it was alive." For a new life has been born and the promise of the Six Hills fulfilled. That new life is personified in the next (and final) chapter in the baby of Helen Schlegel and Leonard Bast, the child who is to inherit Howards End, who is symbolic of the connection made among all the characters, and who symbolizes as well, as he plays in the hayfield, the man who has found place, who has not lost relation to earth.

And it is place after all that is of supreme importance in the novel—not the generalized background of nature in tinseled poesy, but a *specific* location to which one belongs and through which he can sense his connection with all else—his ancestors, the earth from whence he and all humanity has come. A major reason that all the Wilcoxes except Ruth are incomplete is that they lack place: in spite of their many belongings, they are homeless. They may possess title to Howards End, to Oniton, to the Ducie Street residence, they may have blueprints drawn and houses built; but they lack a sense of belonging to any place. At Oniton:

Day and night the river flows down into England, day after day the sun retreats into the Welsh mountains, and the tower chimes, "See the Conquering Hero." But the Wilcoxes have no part in the place, nor in any place. It is not their names that recur in the parish register. It is not their ghosts that sigh among the alders at evening. They have swept into the valley and swept out of it, leaving a little dust and a little money behind.

So it is, in contrast, that Howards End and all the objects associated with it, including the Six Hills, become recurrent, ever-developing images in the novel, to suggest again and more fully again what never could be defined otherwise, the mysterious power of place. "It is sad to suppose that places may ever be more important than people," Margaret Schlegel says to her sister. "The more people one knows the easier it becomes to replace them. It's one of the curses of London. I quite expect to end my life caring most for a place"; and what she is beginning to realize is what makes her the spiritual heir of Ruth Wilcox: that place may help bring us to the underlying love that is far deeper even than the love of human beings for each other; and that, without place, personal love becomes difficult or impossible, for it is place which can impart to life the sense of "the past sanctifying the present; the present . . . declaring that there would after all be a future."

There exists, as Margaret knows in her moment of resignation, that "deeper stream" of reality, which, in its flow, represents continuity; and Howards End and its wych-elm and hayfield can make known to those who are in kinship with them that the present moment is related to all time, and that past and present and future flow inevitably and forever into the commingling sea.

So, to Helen and Margaret, united finally at Howards End,

the present flowed by . . . like a stream. The tree rustled. It had made music before they were born, and would continue after their deaths, but its song was of the moment. The moment has passed. The tree rustled again. Their senses were sharpened, and they seemed to apprehend life. Life passed. The tree rustled again.

The above comments begin to suggest what is integral to the rhythmic imagery of the novel: that the imagery of Howards End, the place, is used in contrast to the nomadic society all about it, the civilization brought to the world in the name of Wilcoxism; and that the Howards End imagery, like the expanding imagery of *The Longest Journey*, has a kind of *flowing* quality to it. The opposing imagery, that of the world beyond the fields of Howards End, has always a motion to it as well, but it is a motion without order, change without observable relation to past or future. London is described again and again as a city in constant agitation,

bricks and mortar rising and falling with the restlessness of the water in a fountain, as the city receives more and more men upon her soil. Camelia Road would soon stand out like a fortress, and command, for a little, an extensive view. Only for a little. Plans were out for the erection of flats in Magnolia Road also. And again a few years, and all the flats in either road might be pulled down, and new buildings, of a vastness at present unimaginable, might arise where they had fallen.

Personal relations, never stable, are even less so in such a society; Margaret, after Ruth Wilcox's death and before her own marriage to Henry, leans over a parapet to watch the ebbing of the Thames and wonders about the ebb within mankind: "Mr. Wilcox had forgotten his wife, Helen her lover; she herself was probably forgetting. Every one moving. Is it worth while attempting the past when there is this continual flux even in the hearts of men?"

Not for nothing is the master image of the whole novel that of water, of rivers and the sea: for water may represent not only continuity and the "deeper stream" and man's merging with the infinite; it may represent, as the passages above suggest, quite the opposite, flux without meaning or purpose, and man may be lost on the sea, a wanderer exiled from peace and from home. An intricate, expanding image that appears on nearly every page, water is utilized by Forster in both connotations, and an indication of the subtlety and cunning of its use is that its effect is made without the reader's awareness being drawn to the image itself. Always life exists in relation to the ceaseless flow, and some people within that flow will have material advantages over others: Margaret and Helen's inheritance allows them to stand on "islands," Margaret realizes, while "most of the others, are down below the surface of the sea."

The characters, however, are normally all voyagers upon that sea, and their voyage, like that of Ulysses, is finally accomplished in spite of all hazards. In a real sense, indeed, the novel is a modern epic: modern in that the heroism consists of slaying the monster within mankind, not in blinding the Cyclops without; an epic in that it is about a people and their destiny, with the guiding deities always present. The wise Ulysses, pacifier of differences among the Greeks, is replaced by Margaret Schlegel, who is aided in her attempt to mediate in the battle between the "inner" and "outer" lives by the mysterious goddess, Ruth Wilcox, who, through place, can transcend all disunity, and by the supernatural figure of old Miss Avery, less a goddess than an immortal spirit.

The ultimate destination of the voyagers is Howards End, sighted frequently but never spiritually reached until the novel's conclusion. There is a wonderfully realized sense of motion, of rising and falling, throughout. Margaret's journey commences in London, at Wickham Place, which gives a sense "of a backwater, or rather of an estuary, whose waters flowed in from the invisible sea, and ebbed into a profound silence while the waves without were still beating." Wickham Place is to be destroyed by those waves; Margaret, now upon them, is taken upward to the crest of the Purbeck Hills, a vantage point where "system after system of our island" can be seen to "roll together," and where she announces her decision to marry Henry Wilcox; [7] down

---

[7] At this juncture, Margaret wonders "at the disturbance that takes place in the world's waters, when Love, who seems so tiny a pebble, slips in. . . . The foundations of Property and Propriety are laid bare, twin rocks; Family Pride flounders to the surface,

again, and then up the long ascent into the Welsh mountains and into the valley where lies Oniton and the ogre of disaster—for here Helen is "seduced" by Leonard Bast and Margaret learns that Jacky Bast has once been Henry's mistress. Then come the resultant storm and battle, the crisis for Henry and Margaret reached on a slope of the Six Hills, which are themselves capable of motion; and, finally, Howards End is reached—the point, as the name indicates, where water meets land. The water is the flux of modern society whereupon they have been tossing, the land the mysterious flow of continuity which is to give them peace.

The repetitive images associated with Howards End, reaching out as they do to imply a merging of present with all time, constitute one of the greatest triumphs of the novel. Hay is the central one of these images, and it becomes one of the flowing images which suggest a unity of present with past and future, the unity which Ruth Wilcox intuitively perceives and which is denied the other members of the Wilcox clan. They, we understand, are allergic to hay; she is associated with it from the moment of her first entrance, an entrance which ends the quarrel precipitated by Aunt Juley's arrival at Howards End. Mrs. Wilcox

---

puffing and blowing, and refusing to be comforted; Theology, vaguely ascetic, gets up a nasty ground swell. Then the lawyers are aroused—cold brood—and creep out of their holes. They do what they can; they tidy up Property and Propriety, reassure Theology and Family Pride. Half-guineas are poured on the troubled waters, the lawyers creep back, and, if all has gone well, Love joins one man and woman together in Matrimony."

approached just as Helen's letter has described her, trailing
noiselessly over the lawn, and there was actually a wisp of hay
in her hands. She seemed to belong not to the young people
and their motor, but to the house, and to the tree that over-
shadowed it. One knew that she worshipped the past, and
that the instinctive wisdom the past can alone bestow had
descended upon her—that wisdom to which we give the
clumsy name of aristocracy. High born she might not be.
But assuredly she cared about her ancestors, and let them help
her.

Margaret's spiritual progression toward Mrs. Wilcox
and Howards End is at least partially conveyed by
Forster through the association of the hay image with
Margaret herself. At the novel's mid-point, she visits
Howards End at Henry's suggestion. On the porch she
picks some weeds and, clutching them in her hand,
enters the house to meet Miss Avery, in years past a
friend of the grandmother of Ruth Wilcox who had
given the house to Ruth; now Miss Avery takes Margaret to be Ruth herself: " 'In fancy, of course—in
fancy. You had her way of walking. Good-day.' And
the old woman passed out into the rain." Margaret still
does not "belong" to Howards End, she has not as yet
achieved it in her spiritual journey, hers are weeds instead of hay; but, as E. K. Brown remarks, the incident
and weeds suggest "that she has more than begun" to
reach toward Ruth.

Later, in the garden at Oniton, Margaret picks up
grass from the mowing machine and lets it pass through
her fingers. She has just learned that Henry, during a
period of his marriage to Ruth, had as mistress Jacky

Bast; and now Margaret and Henry are discussing the affair, Henry beginning to color it in as favorable a shade as possible, unable to see that the "really culpable point" has been "his faithlessness to Mrs. Wilcox." But Ruth Wilcox "would pity the man who was blundering up and down their lives"; and Margaret, as Ruth must in silence have done, forgives. Going to her room after the conversation, she leaves a "long trickle of grass . . . across the hall."

Margaret will never attain the full knowledge she attributes to Ruth Wilcox; but what Margaret has learned is that she may gain help from Ruth, buried in the Hilton graveyard, as Ruth had gained help from her ancestors. The hay, the grass, now symbolizes Margaret's own connection with the past; but she has not as yet achieved peace. Caught in the turmoil of events which has not even ended with the death of Leonard Bast, Margaret wonders what has become of the "true selves" of the people involved, for their values seem to be the result only of cause and effect. "Here Leonard lay dead in the garden, from natural causes; yet life was a deep, deep river, death a blue sky, life was a house, death a wisp of hay, a flower, a tower, life and death were anything and everything, except this ordered insanity."

Human existence and personal relations are more than "ordered insanity," and Margaret's horror is not to be lasting; for even in the moment of horror, the images which have come to her are, though seemingly fragmentary and unrelated, true ones, images of the underlying continuity which can impart meaning to those relations. In terms of the novel, life is a river *and* a house. Like Ansell's cow in *The Longest Journey*, which has its own existence and reality whether anyone is there to see it or not, the house has its own existence; to Helen, "a surer life than we, even if it was empty." For the house, like its wych-elm and vine,[8] is of the present and yet in the ceaseless flow, forever making contact both forward and back. Margaret will feel, in spite of all contrary evidence, "that our house is the future as well as the past." Miss Avery, indeed, is the "heart" of the house, as we know from Margaret's first meeting with her. Margaret, entering the house alone, hears a reverberation: "It was the heart of the house beating, faintly at first, then loudly, martially"; and,

[8] The wych-elm figures prominently, in the passages earlier mentioned and elsewhere, as a symbol of the promise which the past holds for the present, as a symbol of what man never can fully decipher—his relation through the mysterious natural flux to all time and to divinity. It recalls the tree of "The Road from Colonus" containing the tiny votive offerings indicative of the divine power which the people of the countryside have found manifested within nature; Mrs. Wilcox tells Margaret that long ago country people put pigs' teeth into the trunk of the wych-elm, "and they think that if they chew a piece of the bark, it will cure the toothache." And it is under the ancient tree that Helen Schlegel and Paul Wilcox embrace.

A less frequent image, the vine relates particularly to the fertility which exists as a primary element in the natural flux. Its most important appearance is at the moment that Margaret, through Henry's trick, manages to meet Helen at Howards End and discovers Helen to be pregnant. Helen "sat framed in the vine, and one of her hands played with the buds."

throwing open the door to the stairs, she sees Miss Avery descending. Howards End, says Margaret to Helen as they find reconciliation at the house, "kills what is dreadful and makes what is beautiful live"; and Miss Avery its heart, its spirit of life, must have the "dreadful" annihilated before she is pacified, before the house can be made again a place for mankind's burgeoning.[9]

Each of the images of Margaret's moment of horror is what she senses it to be, yet each contains its opposite as well. In one sense, hay is death, as is the blue sky, for hay, like sky, betokens unity and peace; one is reminded of the funeral of Ruth Wilcox, when, after the burial, after the woodcutter has stolen a flower from the grave for his girl, clouds pass over the graveyard from the west, and the "church may have been a ship, high-prowed, steering with all its company towards infinity." Sky, Margaret's death image, thus comprehends all life images as well, being equally a flowing; and sky, hay,

[9] Miss Avery tells Margaret that Ruth Howard should have married not Henry Wilcox but "some real soldier," and it is Miss Avery who hangs among the books at Howards End the naked sword of Mr. Schlegel, Helen and Margaret's father, who had been both soldier and idealist, embodiment of the life of action and the life of imagination. The error of the marriage is not rectified until, with the death of Leonard Bast, brought about by a heart attack as Charles Wilcox hits him with the flat of the sword, the "dreadful" is killed within Henry, connection is made between Henry and Margaret, and the baby son of Helen and Leonard comes to live in the home he is to inherit. Thus there is a fuller implication than the obvious in Miss Avery's remark after Leonard has fallen: " 'Yes, murder's enough,' said Miss Avery, coming out of the house with the sword."

flower, river, and house are each separate but together, as life and death are part of the same stream: grass withered today "will," as Margaret says to Helen in the epilogue, "sweeten tomorrow."

For Margaret is soon to be aware of the connection among the separate images of her moment of horror; and so it is, at the end, that the hay image, emphasized so strongly, is intended to incorporate the basic meaning—continuity, the eternal, unifying movement of rebirth through death—of each of the other flowing images associated with Howards End. Each image is individual, yet each is part of all; it is the point that is so beautifully made, too, by the recurrent image of the moon in the chapters which bring Leonard from London to meet his death at Howards End. The moon, whose "bright expanses . . . a gracious error has named seas," is shining equally on Germany and on London and Howards End; at Howards End, it causes the house to enshadow "the tree at first, but as the moon rose higher the two disentangled, and were clear for a few moments at midnight"—a few moments of exquisite peace, when each has its separate identity beneath the serene light of unity. And the lesson that Margaret will preach to Helen at the novel's summation is much the same: individual differences needn't be a cause for worry, indeed they are "planted by God in a single family, so that there may always be colour; sorrow perhaps, but colour in the daily grey."

The picture drawn of Margaret in this last chapter is not a singularly sympathetic one. Even if she has achieved a partial identification with Ruth Wilcox, even if she has become qualified as a spiritual heir of Howards End, she still is not the one selected to connect present with future through her progeny. Hers is but ownership of Howards End until Helen's child shall assume possession, and, with the completion of her major task of connection, there only remains for her the nursing of Henry Wilcox and the careful maintenance of the property. Though the flow continues, there is a pedantry and a curious immobile quality in the childless Margaret, who keeps jealous watch of Howards End for Helen's son: she gives "a little cry of annoyance" when Paul Wilcox's foot strikes the front door, for she doesn't "like anything scratched"; and she stops "in the hall to take Dolly's boa and gloves out of a vase." Even, indeed, when the scything of the hay in the meadow begins, she takes off her pince-nez the better to observe; for she and Helen together form the whole unit, and it is Margaret who is observer now, Helen and her baby son who are associated with the hay, with the flow of continuity. Accordingly, Helen's are the last words of the novel, and they concern the completion of one phase in that flow; bursting into the room where Margaret has just heard from Henry that it was Ruth Wilcox's wish that Margaret inherit Howards End, Helen cries: "The field's cut! . . . We've seen to the very end, and it'll be such a crop of hay as never!"

It is unfortunate that so much unfinished business must be resolved in this last chapter; Margaret, Henry and Helen busy themselves at it, but one has the sensa-

tion that all of them, even Helen, are fading in importance before the fact of the stream itself. And so it is
that the effect of *Howards End*, when one thinks back
upon the novel, is that of ceaseless motion. In the initial
portion, it is a motion mainly without direction or reason; that chaotic turbulence is gradually supplanted, as
the novel progresses, by a motion within order; and, at
the conclusion, a sense of that latter motion, the flowing
of the stream of continuity, carries onward far beyond
Helen's cry that the season's hay has been cut. A flow
without beginning or end, passing from horizon to
horizon, forever rising and falling, yet mysteriously
serene, mysteriously ordered: this is the "larger existence" which begins to form as the novel moves from
mid-point to conclusion; this is the "difficult" rhythm
it possesses after it has been read.

A Passage to India

Yet, after this has been said, it must be added that
Howards End does not achieve nearly the degree of
final liberation and expansion *A Passage to India*
does. The reason it does not concerns the problem of
voice and has been discussed in the preceding chapter;
briefly, again, the lesser expansion of *Howards End* relates to a never-resolved conflict between the detached
position of the Forsterian voice and the position of
Margaret Schlegel, actively engaged as she is within the
world of human relations. In *A Passage to India*, the
disparity between the positions is acknowledged from
the opening chapters; the encompassing power of God-

bole's love is gained from as great a denial of his own consciousness as he can make, and from his accompanying detachment from the physical reality. The greatest extent of the encompassment of his love is that point at which he can successfully abnegate no further his own consciousness; in a passage already quoted, he displays his ability to love equally Mrs. Moore and a wasp, but he cannot love equally the stone on which the wasp is found: "he had been wrong to attempt the stone, logic and conscious effort had seduced, he came back to the strip of red carpet and discovered that he was dancing upon it."

To discover more fully the reason that Godbole's sense of love, though incomplete, not only remains undisturbed but finally—as the passage above indicates—encompasses all that the defeated Mrs. Moore ever represented, it is necessary to consider the major image of *A Passage to India* and the most provocative image of all of Forster's novels—the Marabar Hills with their countless caves. Mystery shrouds the caves throughout; that they are "extraordinary" we know from the first sentence of the novel, but as to what makes them so we are never precisely told. Godbole, who knows their secret, won't reveal it. At Fielding's tea party, Aziz, partly for the entertainment of Adela Quested and Mrs. Moore, attempts to make Godbole discuss the caves, but "the comparatively simple mind of the Mohammedan was encountering Ancient Night." It is impossible, Forster suggests, to explain the unique nature of the caves: "Nothing, nothing attaches to them, and their reputation—for they have one—does not depend upon human speech. It is as if the surrounding plain or the passing birds have taken upon themselves to exclaim 'extraordinary,' and the word has taken root in the air, and been inhaled by mankind."

Yet gradually the implications of the image become clearer, though initially not so much through specific description as through the effect the hills and caves produce on three of the major characters—Mrs. Moore, Adela, Fielding. A voice, "very old and very small," speaks to Mrs. Moore in one of the caves and completely demolishes her sense of values; she accepts a total negation and doesn't "want to communicate with anyone, not even with God." In another cave, Adela undergoes the illusion that Aziz has attempted her seduction, an illusion strong enough to cause her severe shock and to send Aziz to trial, the trial which affords the structural climax of the novel. An echo produced by the emptiness and smallness of the caves—and the echo is to become one of the major expanding images of the novel—is central to the effect the caves have on both Adela and Mrs. Moore. To Fielding, it is not the interior of the caves (he is unaffected there) but the distant view of them at sunset from the verandah of the club at Chandrapore that disturbs:

It was the last moment of the light . . . they seemed to move graciously towards him like a queen, and their charm became the sky's. At the moment they vanished they were everywhere, the cool benediction of the night descended, the stars sparkled, and the whole universe was a hill. Lovely, exquisite

moment—but passing the Englishman with averted face and
on swift wings. He experienced nothing himself; it was as if
someone had told him there was such a moment, and he was
obliged to believe.

Later, "fatigued by the merciless and enormous day,"
he experiences a similar sensation

He lost his usual sane view of human intercourse, and felt that
we exist not in ourselves, but in terms of each others' minds
—a notion for which logic offers no support and which had
attacked him only once before, the evening after the catastrophe, when from the verandah of the club he saw the fists
and fingers of the Marabar swell until they included the whole
night sky.

Obviously, in the description of hills and caves,
Forster, as E. K. Brown says, "is taking his characters
beyond their depth"; their minds, "Western, modern,
complex, cannot operate on the level of primitivism
which the hills and the caves exemplify." Yet the implications have been such that we can come to somewhat
closer terms with the Marabar than this. Fielding's
reaction suggests, certainly, that the hills represent some
kind of unifying reality. The vastness of that transcendent unity is to him not only incomprehensible but
disturbing: an agnostic, he lives wholly within the
rational, phenomenal world, and his primary concern
within that world is that of human relationships; the
hills have imparted to him the sensation that the reality
of that world is essentially illusory.

The vastness, so troubling to Fielding, is something
which Mrs. Moore, of course, has always accepted; she

is aware of the huge expanse beyond the phenomenal world and of a divine unity encompassing that expanse. Yet the effect made upon her within the cave is quite the reverse of that made upon Fielding as he views the hills from Chandrapore: for her, indeed, "the Marabar . . . robbed infinity and eternity of their vastness, the only quality that accommodates them to mankind." The reason the Marabar produces dissimilar effects upon Fielding and Mrs. Moore is related to the difference in their intuitive powers. For certainly hers is much greater than his and is not so extensively limited as is his by the reasoning faculty. If momentarily the Marabar has caused Fielding to sense a greater reality which threatens his conception of the phenomenal world as the only reality, it has caused Mrs. Moore to become aware, if but inadequately, of a transcendent principle which goes far beyond the divine reality which she has always perceived—so far beyond, in fact, that her whole scheme of values based upon that divine reality is demolished.

Mrs. Moore, until she enters the cave, has perceived a God who exists in the universe and who, possessing the attribute of good, is ever aware of any divergency from that attribute. The spaciousness of the Indian night sky increases her awareness of the divine unity, and she senses the spiritual flow connecting her with the universe:

In England the moon had seemed dead and alien; here she was caught in the shawl of night together with earth and all the other stars. A sudden sense of unity, of kinship with the heavenly bodies, passed into the old woman and out, like water through a tank, leaving a strange freshness behind.

It is the moment, we are told later, that India had "seemed to her good." In *Howards End*, Ruth Wilcox is aware of that good, of that unifying love, through the sense of the spiritual flow afforded by earth: the spirits of the dead, of all the human past, are operating through her to harmonize human and divine. Like Ruth Wilcox, Mrs. Moore is intuitively aware of the supernatural; but no ghosts reside in the Marabar, no spirits of the past to aid and abet the present. To call the hills "uncanny" misleads, Forster is careful to state, for " 'uncanny' suggests ghosts, and they are older than all spirit." Not only are they older than, and hence without, spirit, but they are devoid of any attributes—empty, indeed, except for the voice that Mrs. Moore hears to her destruction. Some of the caves have entrances, some of them do not; it is the only difference which can be discerned. The caves without entrances have not been "unsealed since the arrival of the gods. . . . Nothing is inside them, they were sealed up before the creation of pestilence or treasure; if mankind grew curious and excavated, nothing, nothing would be added to the sum of good or evil."

What, then, happens to Mrs. Moore in the cave? To put it simply, it is the case of her intuitive apparatus going blank, for there is *nothing* for it to receive—nothing, that is, except the voice she hears, "something snubnosed, incapable of generosity—the undying worm itself." On the literal level, that voice is the echo which is produced following the striking of a match: the sound

THE NOVELS OF E. M. FORSTER

"starts a little worm coiling, which is too small to complete a circle but is eternally watchful." On the metaphysical level, the voice is suggestive of the transcendent principle of the Marabar: before time and space, devoid of attributes, the empty absolute. Such a concept of the absolute is not foreign to the Hindu philosophical systems; in the metaphysics of the Vedanta, the doctrinal basis of all Hinduism, Brahman, the absolute reality, is without attributes, without distinctions. Nothing can be ascribed to it, nothing said of it: it is unknowable.

As an echo, the voice cannot *be* the absolute; nor can Mrs. Moore, in hearing the echo, have achieved total identification with the absolute. There would be, one assumes, no echo at all, had total identification been made; at the conclusion of the novel, as Forster brings his themes together in a triumphant finale, he describes a single crack of thunder which has no accompanying echo: it is the suggestion of a completed union. Although Mrs. Moore's vision in the cave is incomplete, the results produced upon her are similar to those produced at the moment of Nirvana when the individual soul (Atman) merges with pure being: to Mrs. Moore, as in the moment of Nirvana, the physical world loses its significance and all distinction, moral as well as physical, is obliterated. Thus the echo brings the destruction of all her values; meaning and importance no longer are to be found in friends, family, the grandchildren to come, the supreme Lord with attributes. Distinctions themselves vanish; the echo has murmured to her,

" 'Pathos, piety, courage—they exist, but are identical, and so is filth. Everything exists, nothing has value.' If one had spoken vileness in that place, or quoted lofty poetry, the comment would have been the same— 'ou-boum.' " The response of Mrs. Moore—who, though she has desired to achieve oneness with the universe, believing the achievement to be "dignified and simple," has not realized that such a quest might lead to total negation—is initially one of "horror"; she feels she is becoming ill. But then, surrendering to the vision, she loses "all interest, even in Aziz, and the affectionate and sincere words that she had spoken to him seemed no longer hers but the air's."

That Forster intends the emptiness of the cave to represent the absolute Brahman and the echo to represent Mrs. Moore's incomplete awareness of that absolute is suggested also by the parallel that exists between the "ou-boum" she hears and the divine symbol "OM" of the Vedas. "This syllable is Brahman. . . . The Self, whose symbol is OM, is the omniscient Lord. He is not born. He does not die. He is neither cause nor effect. This Ancient One is unborn, imperishable, eternal." [10]

Following the experience in the cave, Mrs. Moore must wait some months before she is permitted to die.

[10] This quotation and others which follow are from the translation of the *Upanishads* by Swami Prabhavananda and Frederick Manchester, now available in a paper-backed edition (Mentor Books, 1957). For a further discussion of the parallel between "OM" and Forster's "ou-boum," see Glen O. Allen's essay on *A Passage to India* (PMLA, December, 1955).

The nature of that experience has caused her to lose interest in *all* reality, whether physical or transcendent. Selfishness, irritability, and self-pity are her characteristics as she returns to the problems and conflicts of the human sphere: "her constant thought was: 'Less attention should be paid to my future daughter-in-law and more to me, there is no sorrow like my sorrow,' although when the attention was paid she rejected it irritably." Love, the quality upon which she had depended, is now derided: "And all this rubbish about love, love in a church, love in a cave, as if there is the least difference, and I held up from my business over such trifles!" she cries, irritated by her responsibility in connection with Ronnie and Adela's forthcoming marriage. It is worth noting that Mrs. Moore's attitude after the Marabar experience finds representation in one member of the Brahmanical triad. Brahma, Vishnu, and Siva represent creation, preservation, and dissolution, respectively. When activity prevails, Brahma is supreme; when goodness, Vishnu; and when apathy, Siva. It is Siva, certainly, who emerges triumphant after Mrs. Moore's vision in the cave; a sense of evil, an absence of good, is the dominant note throughout most of the central section of the novel.

Yet it is appropriate here to recall Forster's suggestion that "apathy, uninventiveness, and inertia" may be required before man can achieve "a sprouting of new growth through the decay"; Mrs. Moore's negating vision is a requisite for any new spiritual growth in a society that has lost contact with earth. That growth, of course, is to be achieved through Godbole, or, at least, through the power of love which he possesses. What, then, is the difference between Mrs. Moore, whose love is destined for failure, and Godbole, whose love is not? A partial answer is provided by an episode that occurs at Fielding's tea party. At that party, Godbole, despite Aziz's attempts, refuses to discuss the secret of the Marabar with Mrs. Moore and Adela Quested. But, as the group is preparing to leave, he agrees to sing for the benefit of the Westerners. The song is "a maze of noises, none harsh or unpleasant, none intelligible." Godbole's explanation of the song, in response to a query by Fielding, is important enough, I think, to quote in its entirety:

"I will explain in detail. It was a religious song. I placed myself in the position of a milkmaiden. I say to Shri Krishna, 'Come! come to me only.' The god refuses to come. I grow humble and say: 'Do not come to me only. Multiply yourself into a hundred Krishnas, and let one go to each of my hundred companions, but one, O Lord of the Universe, come to me.' He refuses to come. This is repeated several times. The song is composed in a raga appropriate to the present hour, which is the evening."

"But He comes in some other song, I hope?" said Mrs. Moore gently.

"Oh no, he refuses to come," repeated Godbole, perhaps not understanding her question. "I say to Him, Come, come, come, come, come, come. He neglects to come."

Krishna, the deity whom Godbole worships, is an incarnation of Vishnu. Together, Krishna-Vishnu and Brahma (representing as they do creativity and goodness) are the Hindu equivalent of the Christian God incarnate, and Forster on several occasions points out the parallels between the Krishna legend and the story of Christ. But Godbole, unlike Mrs. Moore, requires no belief that God can come to him; unlike Mrs. Moore, he does not even need to sense the principle of good in the world about him. "Good and evil," he tells Fielding as they discuss the Marabar incident,

are different, as their names imply. But, in my own humble opinion, they are both of them aspects of my Lord. He is present in the one, absent in the other, and the difference between presence and absence is great, as great as my feeble mind can grasp. Yet absence implies presence, absence is not non-existence, and we are therefore entitled to repeat, 'Come, come, come, come.'

Come, come: the repetition of the word occurs throughout the novel and serves as one of the rhythmic devices. To Godbole, union with God is always a desire, not a reality; as the Marabar incident has indicated, to achieve Him would inevitably mark the end of love. Thus Godbole not only refuses to discuss the caves, he will avoid the trip to them by making such extensive prayers that he misses the train. Even Godbole's worship of Krishna, a god with attributes, is a token of his separation from ultimate reality; for, though Krishna provides an object for adoration, clearly no *logical* connection can be made between Him and the absolute, which is, of course, without object.

To reach upward through Krishna toward the absolute, all possible barriers must be crossed, the barrier of logic among them: "God si love," one of the inscriptions to Him, "composed in English to indicate His universality," reads at Mau; and the transposition suggests the required separation from the order which reason imposes. The inscription reminds us of, and is a comment upon, Mrs. Moore's "God . . . is . . . love"; for even though the universe never has been "comprehensible to her intellect," still that universe with its planets and stars seems a rational and perceivable complement to her intuited sense of divine order. But in spite of the divorce from rational order, Godbole cannot fully bridge the gap between Krishna and the metaphysical absolute. Krishna affords the means whereby the absolute may be approached, but since He is a token of that absolute, an object, He is finally illusory.[11] Representations of Him, thrown into the water at Mau, far from symbolizing the absorption into the infinite, are but "emblems of passage; a passage not easy, not now, not here, not to be apprehended except when it is unattainable: the God to be thrown was an emblem of that."

---

[11] "This lower knowledge of the Brahman 'with attributes' has its reward. The soul that has attained it takes at death the way of the gods to heavenly bliss, and progresses by stages toward true knowledge and final deliverance." It cannot, however, bring salvation by itself, "for at bottom it is not knowledge but ignorance which ascribes attributes and personality to Brahman, and sets him, as creator and ruler, over against a world of finite reality, and above all, conceives him as another and a stranger to the soul itself" (George Foot Moore, *History of Religions* [New York, 1916]).

Since the absolute is beyond the categories of time and space, since it is before creation (before Brahma in Hindu theology), it is only by the fullest possible remove from the phenomenal world that it can even be approached. Too, the seeming existence of the phenomenal world which the consciousness perceives must be, in relation to the absolute, illusory; for that matter, the phenomenal world *and* consciousness itself are, in the metaphysical sense, nonexistent.[12] Godbole hence moves in the direction taken by Mrs. Moore as a result of her vision in the cave: it is a movement toward self-abnegation, toward the denial of individuality.

What must be stressed is that Mrs. Moore's love cannot exist in a world from which good is absent: the presence of good is evidence to her of God's existence. In spite of her intuitive ability, she requires a divine order perceivable to her reason. India represents a world from which order has disappeared; it is a world in which good itself is no longer to be found. Mrs. Moore's love —representing the values of western Christianity—is doomed; Godbole's—requiring none of the foundations upon which her love is built, existing upon nothing beyond itself, finding reason to be a handicap rather than an aid—is the only kind of love which can survive in the world that Forster depicts.

[12] Thus Fielding, looking toward the Marabar, is depressed by the feeling that people exist only in terms of each other's minds, that the individual reality is but a mirror's reflection; thus the members of Aziz's party, nearing the base of the hills, find that all they see is "infected with illusion."

The Marabar, complex image that it is, has further meaning in the novel. Stone is part of that image. And it, like so many of the symbolic and thematic elements in the novel, bears a close relationship to Hindu philosophy. All mind and matter is, according to the *Bhagavad-Gita*, composed of three forces—sattwa, rajas, and tamas. In any given object in the physical world, one force predominates. In a block of granite, tamas, the force of solidity and resistance, predominates; tamas is the obstacle preventing the form in which it is found from achieving its pure essence, its pure state. In *A Passage to India*, stone—the granite of the Marabar as well as the stone on which the wasp rests—represents the point where humanity must inevitably fail in its attempt to become one with the universe. Stone hence remains symbolic throughout the novel of man's inability to obtain completion.[13] Thus Godbole is un-

[13] In commenting on faults of style in Forster, F. R. Leavis points to one of the references to stone as an example of a characteristic stylistic lapse. The passage he chooses is that in which Fielding and Hamidullah discuss the death of Mrs. Moore, and Forster interposes to comment:

"If for a moment the sense of communion in sorrow came to them, it passed. How indeed is it possible for one human being to be sorry for all the sadness that meets him on the face of the earth, for the pain that is endured not only by men, but by animals and plants, and perhaps by the stones?"

The words "plants, and perhaps by the stones" cause Leavis to "reflect how extraordinary it is that so fine a writer should be able, in such a place, to be so little certain just how serious he is." Forster's use of stone here is, however, in perfect keeping with the implications of the stone symbolism. For the passage suggests not only the Hindu idea of the presence of Brahman in

successful in attempting to love the stone equally with the wasp and Mrs. Moore. He has succeeded in overcoming consciousness to the extent that he cannot distinguish his existence from that of other humanity or even from that of an insect; but he has not overcome it to the extent that his existence becomes indistinguishable from that of stone, which has no biological life. "Logic and conscious effort" seduce him back to the state of consciousness—in other words, to that form of existence wherein he distinguishes himself from other existence.

This relation of Godbole to stone, his inability to surmount consciousness to achieve identity with stone and hence with all the universe, is paralleled most beautifully by the symbol of the match flame within the caves. When a visitor to the caves strikes a match,

immediately another flame rises in the depths of the rock and moves toward the surface like an imprisoned spirit: the walls of the circular chamber have been most marvellously polished. The two flames approach and strive to unite, but cannot, because one of them breathes air, the other stone. A mirror inlaid with lovely colours divides the lovers, delicate stars of pink and grey interpose, exquisite nebulae, shadings fainter than the tail of a comet or the midday moon,

---

all matter, even stone, but clearly and unobtrusively conveys the human difficulty of rational acceptance of this philosophy. One might compare the passage above with another which involves an even greater "uncertainty" in dealing with the existence of stone. As Adela Quested and Aziz ascend the Marabar Hills, "the air felt like a warm bath into which hotter water is trickling constantly, the temperature rose and rose, the boulders said, 'I am alive,' the small stones answered, 'I am almost alive.'"

all the evanescent life of the granite, only here visible. . . .
The radiance increases, the flames touch one another, kiss,
expire. The cave is dark again, like all the caves.

The passage, of course, is capable of many interpreta-
tions. That this is so is undoubtedly one of the reasons
for its fascination for the reader and for its success in
the context of the novel. Is the match flame, which
"breathes air," to be taken as the conscious life spirit?
Probably so. It is also Atman, the individual soul,
which is one with Brahman. Atman, the *Katha-
Upanishad* tells us, "dwells forever in the heart of all
beings"; he has "entered the cave of the heart, the
abode of the Most High." Further, Atman "is like a
flame without smoke"; and the same Upanishad goes
on to comment that "in one's own soul Brahman is
realized clearly, as if seen in a mirror." In the Forster
passage, the granite of the cave is expanded to imply
the matter of the phenomenal universe; the reflection
of the flame would be the Brahman that dwells in the
stone, in all of the universe. But the phenomenal universe is but a mirror—the image holds not only in the
passage, but elsewhere in the novel—and the existence
of the identical flame in the wall is actually illusion.
Union of Atman and Brahman can be achieved only
by the extinction of consciousness, by the expiration
of the match flame. It is once again the moment of
Nirvana (the word, in fact, refers to the "blowing
out" of the flame of life), when the individual soul
divorces itself finally from consciousness and all illusion and merges with the absolute.

In the cave symbology, then, Forster has accomplished an intricate, multiple functioning which binds the whole novel together in a way hardly short of the miraculous. In terms of plot, the caves provide the basis for Adela's accusation of Aziz; in terms of meaning, they represent a multiplicity of thematic strands. They represent the complete divorce of human spirit from earth, a statement of man as alien on earth. They suggest the impasse which western civilization has reached: in his separation from earth and in his inability to find divinity in the cosmic motion, man has unwittingly reached a spiritual negation. Yet the caves suggest, too, that a reality exists beyond time and space to which man's consciousness cannot fully reach, and to which that consciousness, even as it reaches out to apprehend ultimate reality, finally is a barrier.

The caves in yet another way symbolize the world in which the characters—and mankind—live. Indeed, the whole universe as it is found in the novel is but one of the Marabar Caves. The circular form of a cave is also the arch of the Indian sky, upon which (as in the grouping of the caves within the hills) is found yet another arch. Where does it all end? The hollow boulder of the Kawa Dol tops all the hills and "mirrors its own darkness in every direction infinitely"; Mrs. Moore, affected by the Indian sky, is aware that "outside the arch there seemed always an arch, beyond the remotest echo a silence." The concept of infinitude in time and space is acceptable only to the extent of one's intuitive power, Forster suggests. When intuition falters or fails, the reaches of time and space—like the transcendent principle within the Marabar—become incomprehensible, empty of meaning: the human mind cannot grasp that which has no apparent beginning or end.

Even as the arch of the cave implies another arch beyond, so the echo of the cave is the echo of all India, of all the world; it is used with consummate effect from the beginning of the novel to the conclusion. The echo, like the mirrored flame of which it is the auditory equivalent, is the product of individual consciousness: it is another sensory impression within the illusory and finite world. Throughout the novel, it signifies the return of sound from circular wall or arching sky, sound reverberating in a world from which good is missing. To Adela, the echo in the cave has released evil. "The sound had spouted after her when she escaped" from the cave and from Aziz, "and was going on still like a river that gradually floods the plain. . . . Evil was loose . . . she could even hear it entering the lives of others." And Fielding will reflect that, unlike in the eighteenth century, "everything echoes now; there's no stopping the echo. The original sound may be harmless, but the echo is always evil."

Yet Forster's use of rhythm—in the earlier novels as well as this one—to imply an order beyond the phenomenal world is in itself the use of a kind of echo; and in *A Passage to India* all the repetitive devices supplement the echo image itself to impart to that image a richness and complexity that go beyond the implication of evil alone. Asirgarh, a fortress town which Mrs.

Moore sees as she journeys across India homeward bound for England, becomes an echo symbol: the town appears, vanishes, reappears. From the train window, she views the town at sunset:

> No one had ever mentioned Asirgarh to her, but it had huge and noble bastions and to the right of them was a mosque. She forgot it. Ten minutes later, Asirgarh reappeared. The mosque was to the left of the bastions now. The train in its descent through the Vindyas had described a semicircle round Asirgarh. What could she connect it with except its own name? Nothing; she knew no one who lived there. But it had looked at her twice and seemed to say: "I do not vanish."

The incident, with its sense of affirmation for Mrs. Moore, is in contrast with the earlier negation produced in her by the echo in the cave. As is true of the caves, nothing attaches to Asirgarh; but now a statement has been made: Asirgarh is there, Asirgarh remains. It marks, unobtrusively, the completion of a cycle for Mrs. Moore and is the moment in the novel (coming even before Adela's withdrawal of her charges against Aziz) when the forces of evil begin to give ground. In terms of the triad, Siva gradually recedes from this point to the conclusion of the novel, to be replaced by Vishnu-Krishna; and the novel ends in that tremendous, noisy celebration of the latter at Mau. Up to this moment, the spirits of the Indian earth have proved themselves to be not the friendly spirits of *Howards End*, but rather the malignant goblins of that novel; one of them, we are told, causes the Nawab Bahadur's car to be wrecked. But Mrs. Moore is to die on this same trip homeward, her ghost "shaken off" as her boat nears Suez and as "the arrangements of Asia weaken and those of Europe begin to be felt"; it is her spirit which is now taken into the Indian earth. Two separate tombs containing her remains are reported to the officials at Chandrapore; Mr. McBryde, the police superintendent,

visited them both and saw signs of the beginning of a cult— earthenware saucers and so on. Being an experienced official, he did nothing to irritate it, and after a week or so, the rash died down. "There's propaganda behind all this," he said, forgetting that a hundred years ago, when Europeans still made their home in the country-side and appealed to its imagination, they occasionally became local demons after death —not a whole god, perhaps, but part of one, adding an epithet or gesture to what already existed, just as the gods contribute to the great gods, and they to the philosophic Brahm.

For, in spite of Mrs. Moore's defeat in the cave, after her death she becomes to the Hindus a diety—one which would have appealed to Ruth Wilcox and which Mrs. Moore herself, before her visit to the caves, would have understood. Mrs. Moore is first invoked as goddess in the Hindus' chant of "Esmiss Esmoor" at Aziz's trial. Such a repetition of sacred names—the repetition is itself a kind of echo—is part of the ceremonies at Mau; and there, when the chant "Radhakrishna Radhakrishna . . . Krishnaradha" changes, Aziz hears "in the interstice . . . almost certainly, the syllables of salvation that had sounded during his trial at Chandrapore." Radha, in Hindu legend, is the favorite wife of Krishna;

thus fully does Forster merge Mrs. Moore into Hinduism and transform her defeat into spiritual rebirth—a return after death which fits the echo pattern and suggests a transcendent order.

Illusory though the existence of the phenomenal universe is in terms of the absolute Brahman, still the sense of the unity of existence within that universe provides a means of approaching, while never reaching, the absolute unity. Godbole and Mrs. Moore—before her Marabar journey—are both able to intuit their oneness with, at least, all that which "breathes air" within the world. The two are inseparably linked through the recurrent image of the wasp, though it has but three major appearances in the novel. Mrs. Moore perceives a wasp on a peg, as she goes to hang up her cloak in her son's house; a wasp is discussed by two missionaries, who appear briefly and only for the sake of that discussion; and, finally, in the passage which has already been mentioned, Godbole recollects, during the Mau rites, a wasp resting on a stone. In its initial appearance, the wasp has mistaken

the peg for a branch—no Indian animal has any sense of an interior. Bats, rats, birds, insects will as soon nest inside a house as out; it is to them a normal growth of the eternal jungle, which alternately produces houses trees, houses trees. There he clung, asleep, while jackals in the plain bayed their desires and mingled with the percussion of drums.

"Pretty dear," said Mrs. Moore to the wasp. He did not wake, but her voice floated out, to swell the night's uneasiness.

The incident, seemingly so trivial, has at once differentiated Mrs. Moore from the English residents at Chandrapore and suggests as well, as E. K. Brown points out, that "there are ordeals ahead to which even Mrs. Moore may be insufficient"—ordeals which the jackals, the drums, the night's uneasiness, so beautifully imply. The Government officials must make sharp distinctions, must make categories, of which the most obvious is that of English and Indian; they would not have understood Mrs. Moore's affinity with a wasp—an affinity which is strengthened by the fact that neither to Mrs. Moore nor to the wasp are those distinctions of the slightest significance. But it is not only in the official capacity that distinctions are significant; it is a melancholy truth, Forster seems to be saying elsewhere in the novel, that human relations seem ever strengthened through division. Thus a little later Adela and Ronnie will commence a reconciliation almost immediately after they quarrel, for they sense their own similarity through the difference that exists between them and the Indians about them. Indeed, one of those differences lies in their ability to examine and categorize, and when they cannot identify a small green bird they are disturbed: "It was of no importance, yet they would have liked to identify it, it would somehow have solaced their hearts."

The second appearance of the wasp occurs in the chapter immediately following Mrs. Moore's discovery of one on the peg; now it is brought up during a conversation between the two missionaries, old Mr. Graysford and young Mr. Sorley. They believe in a more inclusive love than do the Government officials. As practicing Christians, they always travel third-class on the railways and spurn the English club; but even the younger missionary who, more advanced, will give a place in heaven to the monkeys, is reluctant to make further concessions:

Jackals were indeed less to Mr. Sorley's mind, but he admitted that the mercy of God, being infinite, may well embrace all mammals. And the wasps? He became uneasy during the descent to wasps, and was apt to change the conversation. And oranges, cactuses, crystals and mud? and the bacteria inside Mr. Sorley? No, no, this is going too far. We must exclude someone from our gathering, or we shall be left with nothing.[14]

The passage suggests the conflict between the quality of infinitude which the Christian gives to God and the immediate limitations which his reason places on that infinitude. The Christian heaven, so far as Mr. Sorley can conceive of it, demands a final exclusion somewhere; and even Mrs. Moore, although she pushes the barriers much farther back than can Mr. Sorley, also must make an exclusion. We have noted that, to Mrs. Moore, all which is good is of God; but when she meets evil—that is, absence of good—in the universe, she cannot reconcile its part in the divine scheme. As she looks at the Ganges in the moonlight—it is the same Indian-

[14] The comment has an implication which is beyond Mr. Sorley; for "nothing," of course, is to be taken also in reference to the absolute reality, Brahman.

moon which has just imparted to her a sense of kinship with the universe, and which, now reflecting on the river, altering and shifting, suggests the flux of nature—she hears from Ronnie of the crocodiles which devour the dead bodies floating down from Benares: "Crocodiles down in it too, how terrible!" she murmurs, and her "gentle creeps" amuse both Ronnie and Adela.

It is a foreshadowing of her destruction within the cave. Yet Mrs. Moore's love of a wasp is not to be finally without meaning, in spite of what happens to her in the Marabar. "Some hundreds of miles westward of the Marabar Hills, and two years later in time, Professor Narayan Godbole stands in the presence of God" at Mau; and it is then that he remembers Mrs. Moore, "though she was not important to him," and successfully impels her, and likewise a wasp, "to that place where completeness can be found."

It was his duty, as it was his desire, to place himself in the position of the God and to love her, and to place himself in her position and to say to the God, "Come, come, come, come." This was all he could do. How inadequate! But each according to his own capacities, and he knew that his own were small. "One old Englishwoman and one little, little wasp," he thought, as he stepped out of the temple into the grey of a pouring wet morning. "It does not seem much, still it is more than I am myself."

The unsolicited appearances to Godbole of the images of Mrs. Moore and wasp exert a powerful force at the conclusion of the novel. For, as E. K. Brown observes, the implication has been made of affinity between Godbole and Mrs. Moore in the very fact that to each a tiny wasp is important; but, even more significantly, the implication has been made that her love has been encompassed by his, the greater of the two.

There are numerous other returns, other rhythmic devices which interweave with the wasp image to give to this last section a sense of order and continuation. "Then you are an Oriental," says Aziz to Ralph Moore, Mrs. Moore's son, who has arrived at Mau with Fielding and Stella; Ralph, like Mrs. Moore before him, has just told Aziz that he can tell whether or not a stranger is his friend. Aziz "unclasped as he spoke, with a little shudder. Those words—he had said them to Mrs. Moore in the mosque in the beginning of the cycle, from which, after so much suffering, he had got free." And the suggestion of course is of the beginning of another cycle, a suggestion made also by the season itself, the season of rain which fills the tanks and allows for the rebirth within nature; made too by the death of the old rajah and the revelation that a child is to be born to Fielding and Stella. There is also the return in these final pages of such images as the birds and snakes, and they are now more easily identifiable; the landscape itself has become less alien, and is "as park-like as England"— although it "did not cease being queer." For harmony between man and his universe has not been fully restored, and man's own completion is as distant and unobtainable as it ever was.

But it is essentially on a note of affirmation that the novel ends. The echo of the caves has been answered

by the tremendous, repeating crashes of sound at Mau:
by the firing of the cannon, the trumpeting of the ele-
phants, the noise of the celebrants, and, drowning all
this, by "an immense peal of thunder, unaccompanied
by lightning," which "cracked like a mallet on the
dome." This latter is a return to the sound within the
caves, to the hollow dome of the Kawa Dol. The single
peal of thunder without lightning is in obvious contrast
to the echo and the flame: it suggests a universe from
which evil has been driven, where consciousness has
been surmounted and unity attained. The thunder is of
course a prefigurement, not a statement of any present
union; or, if it is a union, it is but of the duration of a
moment. As the novel ends, sky, that mirror of the
universe, and rock, that point where man must inevitably fail in his attempt to merge with the ultimate reality, join with the rest of the phenomenal universe to
deny friendship now between Aziz and Fielding; and
the implication is made that complete union will never
be attained until the confines of time and space are finally demolished:

But the horses didn't want it—they swerved apart; the earth
didn't want it, sending up rocks through which riders must
pass single file; the temples, the tank, the jail, the palace, the
birds, the carrion, the Guest House, that came into view as
they issued from the gap and saw Mau beneath: they didn't
want it, they said in their hundred voices, "No, not yet," and
the sky said, "No, not there."

A Passage to India is not only Forster's greatest novel,
but one of the outstanding literary accomplishments of

157

the twentieth century. In it, Forster has wedded the rhythmic devices of music—the return again and again, with variations, of a theme—more perfectly to prose than he has ever managed before, and he has even utilized that return itself (in the form of the echo) as one of the major expanding images of the novel. The novel achieves, more fully than any other he has written, the final expansion for which he has always sought, the expansion which is the novel as a whole and which occurs within the reader after the novel has been finished. Such an expansion is produced by Beethoven's Fifth Symphony, we have earlier noted Forster as saying, "mainly (though not entirely) by the relation between the three big blocks of sound which the orchestra has been playing." The three sections of *A Passage to India* correspond to three such blocks, as E. K. Brown points out, the initial chapter in each section serving to introduce the basic themes which are to follow.

The first section, like its introductory chapter, deals with the vastness of space, and with a sky which "settles everything . . . because it is so strong and so enormous"; it is an immensity in which God is still discernible, though there is increasing difficulty in perceiving Him, and in which the Marabar Caves are still an unknown quality, mysterious and faintly ominous. In the second section, the universe has become a cave, and a cave in which God—the god of love and goodness—is missing; evil is released, and only as the section draws to a close does that evil begin to recede. The final section, in its deafening and joyful noise and in the complexity with which all the major themes of the first two sections are woven into it, is reminiscent of the conclusion of some heroic symphony. The whole pattern is, again as Brown remarks, the "rise-fall-rise" that Forster finds in the novel which for him has always achieved the greatest degree of liberation and expansion, *War and Peace*.

Yet, though such a pattern undoubtedly is a contributing factor in the expansion of *A Passage to India*, it is not the major cause. The major factor in the expansion lies in the fact that, for the first time, Forster has realized that his two commitments—one to the world of human reality, the other to the mid-point between that reality and the transcendent reality beyond—can never be brought fully and satisfactorily together. Fielding and Godbole are separate and must remain so. Fielding's clarity of reason, his desire to achieve brotherhood among men, his acceptance of the physical world as "reality": these are not only desirable qualities, but necessary ones. Yet in a world of spiritual disintegration, a world upon whose surface man is a stranger, a wanderer without home, the qualities of a Fielding will bring no new integration: they make the earth no less hostile, they impart no sense of connection between man and that which is more than man. Granted the contemporary condition as Forster describes it, the way of Godbole is the only possible way: love, even though to exist it must maintain a detachment from the physical world and human relationships, offers the single upward path from the land of sterility and echoing evil. And Godbole, more than any other character in the novels, is, as we have seen, the Forsterian voice itself.

So, for the first time in all the novels, the voice is compatible with the theme. Forster, in the pages of *A Passage to India*, has comprehended finally his own problem and come to terms with it. The long silence which has followed the publication of the novel is an indication that he has found those terms to be as satisfactory as possible.

Bibliography

1. Novels and Short Stories

Dates are those of first publication. Brackets enclose the names of present American publishers.

Where Angels Fear to Tread. London, 1905. [Knopf.]
The Longest Journey. London, 1907. [New Directions.]
A Room with a View. London, 1908. [New Directions.]
Howards End. London, 1910. [Knopf.]
The Celestial Omnibus and Other Stories. London, 1911.
A Passage to India. London, 1924. [Harcourt, Brace; also available in Modern Library edition.]
The Eternal Moment and Other Stories. London, 1928.
Collected Short Stories. London, 1947. [Published in the United States as *The Collected Tales of E. M. Forster*, Knopf.]

2. A Select Bibliography of Critical Studies

Allen, Glen O. "Structure, Symbol, and Theme in E. M. Forster's *A Passage to India*," *PMLA*, December, 1955.

Annan, Noel. "Books in General," *The New Statesman and Nation*, October, 1944.

Ault, Peter. "Aspects of E. M. Forster," *The Dublin Review*, October, 1946.

Belgion, Montgomery. "The Diabolism of E. M. Forster," *The Criterion*, October, 1934.

Brown, E. K. *Rhythm in the Novel*. Toronto. 1950.

——. "The Revival of E. M. Forster," *The Yale Review*, June, 1944.

Burra, Peter. "The Novels of E. M. Forster," *The Nineteenth Century and After*, November, 1934.

Cecil, Lord David. *Poets and Story-Tellers*. London, 1949.

Connolly, Cyril. *Enemies of Promise*. New York, 1948.

Dobrée, Bonamy. *The Lamp and the Lute: Studies in Six Modern Authors*. London, 1929.

Doughty, Howard N., Jr. "The Novels of E. M. Forster," *The Bookman*, October, 1932.

Harvey, John. "Imagination and Moral Theme in E. M. Forster's *The Longest Journey*," *Essays in Criticism*, October, 1956.

Hoare, Dorothy M. *Some Studies in the Modern Novel*. London, 1938.

Holt, Lee Elbert. "E. M. Forster and Samuel Butler," *PMLA*, September, 1946.

Johnstone, J. K. *The Bloomsbury Group*. New York, 1954. Contains a bibliography.

Leavis, F. R. *The Common Pursuit*. London, 1952.

Macaulay, Rose. *The Writings of E. M. Forster*. New York, 1938. Contains a bibliography.

Richards, I. A. "A Passage to Forster," *The Forum*, December, 1927.

Shahani, Ranjee G. "Some British I Admire, V: Mr. E. M. Forster," *The Asiatic Review*, July, 1946.

Swinnerton, Frank. *The Georgian Scene*. New York, 1934.

Trilling, Lionel. *E. M. Forster*. Norfolk, Conn., 1943. Contains a bibliography.

Warner, Rex. *E. M. Forster* (supplement to *British Book News*). London, 1950. Contains a bibliography.

Warren, Austin. *Rage for Order*. Chicago, 1948.

Zabel, Morton Dauwen. *Craft and Character in Modern Fiction*. New York, 1957.

Index